#GodisSTILLgood

#wearestillwinning

Nancy Boyd

To contact the author about speaking at your conference or church please email: pastorn1975@gmail.com

Edited by Sasha Boyd and Eileen Abe-Mesias

ISBN: 978-0-9881977-2-5

Printed in the United States of America

Endorsements

I have had the privilege of knowing Nancy for many years, and I admire how she lives her life and how she leads others.

In #God is STILL Good, Nancy relates the real and raw journey with her husband Bert's diagnosis and subsequent fight with stage four pancreatic cancer. She shares her personal process of facing difficult questions and battling disappointment, yet all the while never losing her unshakable belief that God is still good. With truth, authenticity, and faith, Nancy inspires us to come closer to a loving Father through Scripture, journaling, the support of family and friends, and the power of prayer.

This powerful book will help you discover the undeniable hope that is available to all of us no matter what we face and no matter the outcome. I highly recommend #God is STILL Good.

Steve Backlund
Associate Director, Bethel Leaders Network
Founder of Igniting Hope

What an honor it is to have my dear friend and colleague, Nancy Boyd, ask me to read and then write an endorsement of her book, "#God is STILL Good".

My wife Lindy and I have had the privilege of being close friends with both Nancy and Bert. Through our relationship, I have observed and experienced many of the events shared in this book. I can tell you that every feeling, joy, fear, laughter, breakthrough and breakdown shared by Nancy is transparent and authentic.

Each page will give you insight and encouragement into the lives of two people in difficult circumstances who allowed Holy Spirit to daily fill them and help them navigate past these many challenges I am particularly encouraged by the Daily Prayer Reminders that give me insight into Nancy's incredible strength, human weakness and desire of MORE of Papa GOOD God. The short chapters are a powerful punch for a morning devotion or afternoon spiritual boost.

Nancy shares that you are not alone in any circumstance, and in every step you can discover that God is STILL good.

Richard Oliver
Apostolic Overseer
The River Revival Fellowship

My two big keys in endurance are (1) understanding this won't last forever, and (2) take the focus off yourself and put it onto somebody else. These are critical in making sure you stay strong and get through any present trial. These are exactly what Nancy does right here in this book.

For everyone who is living between the promise and a problem, this is for you. For everyone dealing with disappointment, this is for you. For everyone who needs hope in the middle of storms and confusion, this is for you.

Ian Carroll
Author and Itinerant
Founder of Building Contenders

We are believers in "the faith". We base our lives upon truth found in "the faith." As we walk out this faith, we encounter unforeseen, unplanned and sometimes nasty situations and circumstances that bring our faith in "the faith" to the forefront. Our journeys have a way of bringing us to the edge of our understanding, our fears, our sufficiency. Life can squeeze us like a tube of toothpaste and what comes out of the tube shows us where we really are in the moment.

Nancy's account of this struggle is honest, open, authentic and faith filled. As you read it you will encounter strength and surrender-not a "giving-up" but a faith filled yieldedness expressed in Nancy and Bert's trusting hearts to serve when they felt on top of the world and when they felt the world on top of them.

When I am afraid, I put my trust in You

Psalm 56:3

It is a joy to walk with faith-filled people!

Al Jones

Senior Pastor

River Bakersfield

I dedicate this book to my husband,
Bert, who inspired me daily;
to my children,
Byron, Sarah, Anthony, and Audrey,
who continue to be my inspiration and joy;
to my brother, Rod, who has been
a constant source of strength
and comfort throughout this journey;
and to Pastor Al Jones who was relentless
in his encouragement to write this book.

But especially to the
hundreds of friends who prayed every day -
Thank You.

Contents

Foreword

In #God is STILL good, Nancy opens the door for you to experience a journey of healing and faith with your loving heavenly Father by sharing her own sacred journey through God's refining fire. At times you will laugh at her transparent vignettes and you will cry with her raw vulnerability. It's a book about hearing God in the midst of pain and uncertainty and about choosing to believe Him. It will likely put a finger on whatever may be hindering your ability to see the goodness of God, while providing insights to navigate these hindrances into new possibilities.

Nancy releases transformational pearls of wisdom that add weighty and significant value to your own journey and she gives practical advice to navigate through life's storms and seemingly unanswered questions. If you are looking for tangible hope to walk with God and others through the valley of the Shadow of death; If you want to be an encourager even when you yourself need encouragement; If you are desiring honest, sage wisdom that will provide bite-sized nuggets of fortified truth and not trite niceties, read this book.

I believe the mark of a really well written book is it continually draws the reader into participating with the author and it irresistibly draws them into the next chapter. Thank you, Nancy, for writing just such a book with brilliance that invites us into your prayer closet and into your heart with honesty, vulnerability and integrity to supply us with courage, healing and deep insight!

This is a book to savor as you allow God more and more access to your heart to change you from within. Enjoy the journey!

Brent Lokker
Author
Always Loved: You are God's Treasure, not His Project

1

In the Beginning

When I began this endeavor, I didn't know how the story would end. I didn't know that my husband of 33 years would succumb to the ravages of pancreatic cancer two years and three months after his diagnosis. I didn't know the last chapter wouldn't end with, "and they lived happily ever after." I fully expected to see the miracle of healing manifest in Bert's body.

Upon his passing, I almost trashed this project. I couldn't comprehend how our lack of breakthrough would inspire anyone. But the Lord has refused to allow me to walk away. He continues to impress upon me that I must share our journey and the revelation of his presence throughout that journey with people who also haven't experienced a breakthrough. Perhaps more importantly, how I've pushed through disappointment, anger, self-recrimination, and doubt to hold onto my love, trust, and faith in God and his goodness.

When tragedy strikes a person or family, we tend to respond in one of two ways - we press in for the comfort of God or pull away from him. Many people blame God and turn away from him in their pain and disappointment. The idea that God is responsible for all things is so deeply ingrained in our culture that this is a fairly typical response from both Christians and non-Christians. However, this can be especially true for performance-based Christians. Too often, I've heard the phrase, "How could this happen to me/us? I've been a good Christian." The result of their disappointment ranges from a loss of trust to the outright rejection of God.

Although faith is powerful, it isn't a vaccination against the evils of the world. We can't afford to have a gospel that is devoid of satan. Otherwise, God gets all the blame for the works of the devil. As we say at our church, I have an enemy, and his name is NOT God. We recognize that God is, indeed, all-powerful but he is not all-controlling. We realize that God is not the source of our problem but the answer. In doing so, rather than turn away from him, we push toward him. I've found that in pressing toward, it's possible to enter a place of deeper intimacy and communion with him. He desires to be "with you" in your trials.

God was with me as I received an outpouring of love and prayer support from friends around the world, primarily through my daily requests for prayer on social media during our struggle and since Bert's death. I can't tell you how important those daily touches became to our faith as we engaged our enemy - cancer. The body of Christ - Jesus "with skin on." However, God has also been with me in the car, at doctors' offices, in a silent house that is utterly empty, in the early morning and late at night in an empty bed. A gentle voice always near, waiting for me to turn and receive comfort in his presence. It's been in this place of intimacy that my understanding of his goodness has grown. Here in the quiet place, he has revealed our potential as his children. I want to share with you the way this good God has come alongside me and shown himself to me in the moments of my deepest pain and grief.

In 2016, my husband, Bert, and I co-pastored a small church in the central valley of California. While I served the church as Senior Leader, Bert supported me. He excelled in the marketplace, bringing integrity and faith to his position in marketing. It is tempting to write reams of praise about him, which would all be accurate and true, but suffice it to say, he was a wonderful husband, father, and child of God; loved by everyone who encountered him. The church we led is a renewal church that embraces a "God is good" theology and regularly sees miraculous healing, provision, and encounters. Since Bert's passing, my son-in-law and daughter are in transition to step into the Senior Leadership role. The vision of the church continues to be a resource of healing in our community and region because we firmly believe it is always God's will to heal.

In December of 2016, Bert developed a cough that I was convinced was pneumonia. Acting like the stereotypical he-man, he resisted going to the doctor, especially since things were particularly busy for him at the office. However, he felt so sick and weak that I was finally able to coax him to schedule an appointment with our family doctor. She agreed that he probably had pneumonia and sent him for x-rays. When they came back clear, she ordered a CT Scan and released him to go home, telling him she would call with the results. It was well after office hours when we received a call from her office asking him to come back that night. You don't have to be a prophet to figure out that kind of phone call is not going to be good news.

Bert was light-hearted and joking on the ride in. He had not absorbed the gravity of the circumstances yet. Meanwhile I was overwhelmed with apprehension. Anytime a doctor calls you in after office hours, it isn't going to be good news. Bert kept saying, "It's going to be OK, I'm ready to die. I know where I'm going." It was exasperating. I wanted to scream, "Good for you! But I'M not ready for you to die! This is supposed to be OUR time. The freedom to travel and enjoy each other is just around the corner. I will be left bereft, alone, empty, and you will be frolicking on clouds? I don't think so!"

I should probably give you a brief history of our relationship, so you have a picture of what Bert meant to me. I don't mean to say that our love is more special than anyone else's, but it is uniquely ours. When we met, I was a damaged and broken single mom with tons of issues and a history of poor choices. I won't go into the sordid details, but I had very little value for myself and never really expected to be valued by anyone else. I had a sketchy understanding of God and Jesus from brief religious encounters as a child. I believed in God; I just didn't know him; I saw him as a weird blend of Santa and Judge. I absolutely did not see myself as being good enough to go to church, but I did pray every night that God would send a man to rescue me from the rigors of single parenting and trying to keep the rent paid.

I would pray, "Lord please send a man to marry me. Make him rich (anyone with good credit and a decent car), make him honor women (not a wife beater), and have a good sense of humor (which he would need in my family). Please let him love my kids like his own and never abuse or molest them."

Just about the time I'd reconciled myself to singleness and celibacy (no more dating), Bert called and asked me out on a date. We had been friends for about five years, but he was happily married and out of bounds. Then his marriage ended, and he called me! Our friendship grew into a passion, and we would often tell each other, "We are so good together. Surely God brought this about." I knew Bert was the perfect answer to my prayer (not the perfect man, the perfect answer). He was just so good. My kids became his kids. He was the best provider, parent, son-in-law, husband, and friend, any woman could hope for, and he loved me.

His love gave me a sense of value. It was because of his loving me that I was able to believe that perhaps Jesus could love me when I encountered him five years later. If Bert had not placed that call, had not seen anything worth loving, I don't know that my heart could've ever believed Jesus saw something worth loving. In that way, this amazing man prepared my heart for the greatest love of all. Recognizing this, I've loved him more than I ever thought possible. He became my best friend, my lover, my protector, and in a way, my savior. I could write a book about how much I love him, but that's not this book, so back to the doctor's office.

When our doctor came into the office, she gave a weak smile and said, "You know it's not good news, or I wouldn't have called you back tonight." She then began explaining the results of Bert's CT Scan. A mass in the tail of his pancreas and at least four more in his liver indicated metastatic cancer. There was also a sizeable benign cyst on his kidney, causing his cough by pressing against his diaphragm. That cyst turned out to be a lifesaver, bringing attention to what is usually a silent killer - pancreatic cancer.

Tears slid down her face as she tried to tell us this was basically a death sentence. Bert, being the man he is, began to comfort her, telling her everything would be OK. I, on the other hand, understood we had to fight this and asked what the next steps were. She asked if we knew what oncologist we would want to go to (we did), she would try to get us in.

When we left her office that night, she hugged us both and told Bert, "I hope to see you again," but her face told us that it was not her expectation. The subsequent diagnosis was stage four pancreatic/squamous cancer - a combination of the disease so rare, our oncologist told us it shows up in only one percent of people with cancer. I won't go into everything that we experienced those first few weeks, the way God opened doors that looked closed or the people he sent to us. I want to encourage you that he faithfully and consistently came alongside us as we were besieged by this insidious enemy called cancer. The devotional readings that follow are a result of experiencing God's presence, goodness, and revelation as we tried to walk out our faith in this conflict with the enemy.

At the conclusion of each chapter, I'm choosing to include how I daily communicated with others and encouraged them to pray for Bert. I hope this models for you what it looks like to reach out to others and to increase the effectiveness of prayer. It's also a way of letting you see more deeply into my journey with God. They are included verbatim so please ignore all the grammatical and spelling errors. Wink and smile.

2
Every Prayer Matters

So they set out and went from village to village, proclaiming the
good news and healing people everywhere. Luke 9:6

After praying with people for healing for over 20 years, I'd seen
enough people get healed to know the value of prayer, but the day
after Bert's diagnosis, I could not make myself reach out. I didn't
want to tell anyone. As if saying the words would make the
diagnosis real. I stayed home, grieving most of the day. It was kind
of like a "circling the wagons" mentality of protecting your own.

It is incredible to me how many people contacted me that day.
"You were on my mind." or " I missed you at that meeting." As
much as I KNEW prayer was powerful, I could not bring myself to
tell them what was going on, and I was just too raw. I put everyone
off, with one exception - my friend Lanell. She messaged me,
asking how Bert was doing. Out of the blue. She is an apostolic
intercessor for the nations, and we had gone to Cameroon together
on mission and gotten fairly close. I knew God was behind it, so I
messaged back what was happening with Bert and asked her to
pray. As she assured me she would, she invited me to join her in
praying for a friend of hers that also needed a miracle of healing.
What a gift! I can't tell you the wisdom behind her request! To get
my mind off of myself and our situation and to press in for someone
else redirected my grief into action.

But it is the next day that set the agenda for us. As I was waking
up, I heard the Lord call my name. "Nancy!" It was direct, not
gentle, but not harsh. "

Yes, Lord," I replied, coming fully awake at his tone.

"Nancy! I've been sending you prayer warriors, and you've been turning them away."

The people who had contacted me the day before flashed through my mind, one after the other. Remembering them caused me also to remember my grief, which came flooding back. Overwhelmed, I pressed in. "Lord, please tell me what to do. Is Bert going to die? I need to know how to go forward."

"No, Bert will not die, but it won't be easy. You need every prayer possible. A mountain of prayer. Every prayer prayed will matter." As he impressed this upon me, I could see a line of demonic beings so long there seemed to be no end. I could see as prayer took the first one out, another would step in its place, and I heard him say, "Some things are bigger than one prayer. Don't quit praying because you think it's a lack of faith to keep praying. Don't quit out of discouragement or pride. Just don't quit." Every prayer would be essential to see the end of that line.   God had given me my strategy, pray, and pray some more. Not begging, not out of desperation, but knowing that every prayer brought us one step closer to seeing a breakthrough. Even if we could not see anything happening physically, he had shown me that every prayer was a blow against an unseen and determined enemy.

I've always believed something happens when we pray. We are, after all, the adopted children of God. We've been made righteous by the blood of Jesus and as James says, "the prayers of the righteous are powerful and effective." That morning God prepared me that we would not get our "suddenly" healing, but he also girded me with this truth: Every prayer prayed by a believer is powerful and effective. Every prayer is a weapon against our enemy. Every prayer accomplishes something in the kingdom. Every prayer is one prayer closer to breakthrough — every prayer matters.

Quite often, our initial response to pain and fear is to withdraw or to hide. It is entirely instinctual, and it is deadly. There is nothing the enemy likes more than to isolate and conquer. The Bible says he is like a roaring lion waiting to devour the weak. If you've ever heard a lion roar up close and personal, you know the first thing you want to do is freeze or run and hide. Don't do it! I want to suggest a counter-strategy to fight back.

First, reach out. You don't have to spill your guts or advertise your drama. Just reach out to a few friends and say something like, "I'm having a rough time with something I can't share. Would you please keep me in prayer?" Obviously, if there are people that you can trust, you can be more forthcoming. If you don't know anyone to ask for prayer, call a local church. You can stay relatively anonymous and still ask for prayer. Don't freeze. Don't hide. Don't wait until you feel better because you probably won't. Reach out. Their prayers will give you the momentum to get moving again and to fight back.

Second, there are times when we may be facing something that seems impossible, or our prayers don't appear to be heard. I suggest you follow Lanell's cue and pray about something or someone else. Try asking God what he wants you to pray. It will shift your focus, and it can break the paralysis that comes with crisis. Even if nothing is happening in your situation, you will find that the discipline that comes with intercession can get you moving again in regards to your struggle. As requested, I prayed for

Lanell's friend daily until the day that she informed me that he had been healed. What a boost to my faith! Something I was praying for saw victory. God reassured me that the prayers of the righteous are indeed powerful and effective.

Third, and perhaps most important, remember that you have an enemy and his name is not God. Don't be obsessed with this enemy. Don't be consumed with seeing him everywhere, that's just unhealthy. Remember that his first and favorite strategy is to separate our affection from our heavenly Father. If he can deceive you into believing that God is the author of your pain, he will. Before you fall for that, ask yourself these questions, "Did Jesus do this to the people he loved? Did Jesus give anyone cancer? Did Jesus cause suffering to teach or discipline?" Jesus is the perfect revelation of the heart of God, and if he didn't do it, neither would his Father.

Prayer Illustration

Heavenly Father, Please show me how to pray this morning. Don't just tell me who but how and why. Reveal your heart for their situation and for mine too. Bless me with a divine strategy for prayer today. In Jesus' name, Amen.

Excerpts from my Facebook timeline:
12/24/16
Daily Prayer reminder
I hope this isn't getting tedious.
I must confess that when someone asks me for prayer, I usually stop and pray right then with them. This isn't because of my bold Faith but because I'm so busy and easily distracted that I'm afraid I will forget to pray later.

So I'm reminding you daily because I know that we all have active lives and prayer for Bert's victory could easily be forgotten amid the many demands of your lives.

Your prayers are a wall of protection and a wellspring of hope for us. They matter! And so, I will continue to remind you because they are powerful and effective! Thank you thank you thank you!

Please press like when you have prayed and feel free to share.

#Prayforbert #winning #godisgood #prayersmatter #ihatethedevil #nevergiveupneversurrender

12/30/2017

Daily Prayer reminder

I'm especially emotional this week, flashing back to last year. I am just so thankful for my husband and his life. Having just passed the one year mark, Bert's doctor is surprised he's still alive and I'm surprised he isn't verified as healed. It's not often, but whenever I get discouraged, God reminds me that every prayer is a blow against the devil. It is by your prayers we have prevailed in this storm. Thank you thank you thank you. You are touching more lives than you can imagine by praying for this father in the faith, Bert Boyd.

Please press like when you have prayed and feel free to share with praying friends or copy and paste.

#prayforBert #godisgood #prayersmatter #winning #oneyeardown34togo #surprisingthedoctorisfun #oneprayerclosertobreakthrough #spiritualfather

2/12/2019

Dear friends,

My sweetie is with Jesus today. Thank you for the 2 years you purchased for us with your faithful and relentless prayers. He was always encouraged by the "likes" and encouraging words. We have felt loved, supported and embraced by so many. I will be laying low today. Thank you for your love.

3
A Divine Strategy

No temptation has seized you except what is common to man. And God is faithful; he will not let you be tempted beyond what you can bear. But when you are tempted, he will also provide a way out so that you can stand up under it. 1 Corinthians 10:13

If you need a tsunami of prayer, what do you do? I asked God that very question. The thought of calling our friends was more than I could face. Almost before I could get the idea formed in my mind, he directed me to Facebook. I was surprised, to say the least, but I didn't argue. I'd asked for a strategy and he'd responded, so I put all my drama out there for the world to see. It made me feel exposed and vulnerable and small.

For all its faults, I must say that social media was the most useful and efficient way to contact as many people as possible in as short a time as possible. It also kept me from having to talk, which was still difficult without breaking down into tears. Having been a pastor for several years I am fortunate to have an extensive network of believing friends all over the world, and I knew if I could be brave enough to put it out there, they would be faithful to pray. The response was immediate and overwhelming. Friends from every walk of life responded to my request for prayer. The effect was instant for both of us. As the day went on, it was as if a fog was lifting and the sun was breaking through. I could breathe a little better. I began to get my wind (and my fight) back.

It was interesting how the devil tried to undermine this plan for the first few weeks. I would write out a long and detailed post updating everyone on what was happening and our latest prayer need, and as I pressed post, the whole thing would disappear. When I began asking people to share with praying friends, the share option vanished. Just little things to wear me down. I was already waking up several times a night, praying for my husband, and one lost post would undo me. However, I persisted. I began writing a post every day to remind people to continue to pray for Bert and to update them on our latest victory or prayer need. I decided to write reminders daily because of my own tendency to pray briefly for what's in front of me and to assume "it is done" unless I've heard otherwise. I was determined to keep him at the forefront of everyone's prayer list.

The Bible says that the temptations or trials we face are typical among people but that God is so faithful he will provide a way out so we can bear it. As much as it felt like it, we were not unique. We were not "special" enough to warrant the devil's particular hatred. He hates everybody. I had several friends who were fighting or had fought cancer or something just as devastating, who had experienced loss or pain or anguish. No, we were undergoing what it is to live in a world that heaven hasn't invaded yet. But God - ever faithful - gave us a way out so we could bear it. A divine strategy to overcome this demonic assignment from hell. I want to encourage you to seek the strategy he has for you. Find some time to be quiet and be honest with yourself and him. "I'm lost; I don't know what to do; I'm overwhelmed." If this is where you are, there's nowhere to go but up. Ask him what to pray for and how to pray for it. Ask him what the next step is - not all the steps - just the next one. The strategy may not be prayer, it may be making declarations, it may be repeating prophetic words spoken over you, it may be to buy my book and read it! The point is when he downloads the strategy, do it. Don't analyze its efficiency or impact. Be obedient. Believe he really is that faithful. This isn't the one situation in the world that has him stumped. He will provide a way out. Just Do It.

Prayer illustration

Heavenly Father, I ask you for a heavenly strategy to overcome the mountain I am facing. I need to know how to take the next step before me. Please show me what to do. Give me wisdom and direction to move forward in spite of what I'm facing. In Jesus' name, Amen.

Excerpts from my Facebook timeline:
12/8/16
I hate to do this in a post but this is the quickest and simplest way to convey this information. It would appear that Bert is battling some form of cancer. They have found a mass in his pancreas and 4 smaller ones in his liver. That is why he has lost so much weight and is so tired. We have not met with any specialists yet. That is coming. I know that this is a blow to all of us. I know your first thought will be "what can I do? " so I will tell you :
1. Pray from a position of victory and hope. God is still good and it is always his will to heal.
2. Never say he "has" this disease. We are "fighting" it! Your words have power.
3. Please don't express sympathy. It steals our hope. Get mad at the devil but don't be sorry to us.
4. PRAY. DECLARE. For victory over disease and death. For strength and restoration. For increased hope. For our finances and the finances of the church.

Please be careful of your words. We are fighting, we don't "have. "

Finally, pray and heal every sick person you encounter. If the devil is coming after us, let's go after him. Do not tell Bert "I am sorry", tell him I am standing with you against this. Pray also that I can talk to people without crying. I do not want to convey any hopelessness for them to latch onto.

I love you and thank you for standing with us.

4

Your Words Create Potential

The tongue has the power of life and death,
and those who love it will eat its fruit. Proverbs 18:21

If people could apprehend how powerful the spoken word is, there would be a lot less careless talking. What we say about or to one another is creating the potential of fulfillment. In the Valley of the Dry Bones, God told Ezekiel to "prophesy" life over the bones. He wanted to illustrate the dynamic of what it looks like when what we say partners with the supernatural. God wasn't merely showing Ezekiel that he could make the dry bones come to life. God was demonstrating to Ezekiel how powerful his prophecy would be to Israel. God impressed upon Ezekiel that he would partner with the very words Ezekiel spoke, resulting in the restoration of Israel. Our words are like seeds packed with potential waiting to germinate in the spiritual. When we speak what we hear from God, we are essentially partnering with him to empower blessings. In the same way, when we fail to take our thoughts captive and allow the enemy to influence our words, we are partnering with his curses. As I've heard it said, "We empower a disempowered devil."

In the healing ministry, one of the most important lessons I learned was in how I talked about the illness. The moment you say, "I'm getting sick," is the moment you come into agreement to get sick. Instead, you say, "I'm fighting a cold." You don't say, "I'm sore from yesterday's workout," you say, "I'm recovering from yesterday's workout." This concept may seem like legalism, but remember, our enemy is a legalist looking to be empowered. After years of study and practice, I've discovered I get sick a lot less often since I started practicing this discipline. When I posted our original request for prayer on Facebook, I knew several of my friends would not have this perspective of the power of their words. I was cautious in how I worded my prayer request and asked that no one say Bert "had" cancer, but rather we were fighting cancer. I knew that their words would be crucial to his healing and victory.

Whether you are fighting disease or talking about your kids, what you say will determine what you empower. Anytime you partner with what God wants you to say, you are releasing a blessing. Alternately, when your words partner with the devil, you will issue a curse. The power of a blessing is higher than the power of a curse because you are partnering with greater power.

Take some time today and invite God to reveal anytime you have inadvertently agreed with the devil over your health, your family, your finances, your career. Repent in each instance. When you have done this, ask God what he has to say about each situation. Speak those thoughts out. You can repeat them several times throughout the day. Just hearing the words will strengthen your faith in his desire to bless you.

Prayer Illustration

Dear Lord, Please make me more aware of what I'm imparting with my words. I want to declare life, not death! Please show me how to partner with you. Help me release your goodness into the lives of the people I encounter today. Reveal to me whenever I inadvertently empower the plans of the devil through thoughtlessness. In Jesus' name, Amen.

Excerpts from my Facebook timeline:

12/29/16

Daily Prayer reminder

A lot of people have sown into my spiritual growth. I have been blessed by lots of teachers but none of them have better equipped me for this particular battle more than Steve and Wendy Backlund. Their teaching on declarations has given us enormous strength and hope.

Every morning Bert and I start our day with 100 declarations of God's promises. We always finish stronger than we start and our spirits are uplifted. I have them posted on our Web page if you would like to join us in declaring God's goodness each day at igogod.org

Today I am declaring something I learned specifically from Wendy "the power of a blessing is greater than the power of a curse. "

Thanks for agreeing with me in prayer today! Thank you thank you thank you! Please press like when you have prayed and feel free to share!

#Prayforbert #prayersmatter #godisgood #beatingthecursecalledcancer #winning #ideclarelife #letsjustlaughatthat

04/11/17

Daily prayer reminder

We just got back from the Hawaii National Volcano Park. Amazing. We stood over fissures in the ground where steam from lava was escaping, walked through lava tubes, and stood at the edge of the crater. It all seemed tranquil but underneath our feet was more power than we could comprehend. The kind of power that changes the landscape when it is unleashed. The kind of power that creates and destroys islands. Impressive. It is the same with prayer. On the surface they may seem tame but our prayers have even greater potential to destroy death and create life. Once they are released, there is no stopping them.

Please keep praying powerful prayers for Bert Boyd. This trip has been the gift of a lifetime but I want more. Please press like when you have prayed and feel free to share with praying friends.

#prayforBert #godisgood #prayersmatter #winning #prayerserupting #prayersflowlikelava #unstoppable #hesworthit

5
Please Press Like
(The Importance of Encouragement)

". . . Be strong and courageous. Do not be terrified; do not be
discouraged, for the LORD your God will be with you
wherever you go." Joshua 1:9

Hopeless. One of the initial reactions to a diagnosis like the one
our doctor gave us was to feel overwhelmed and lost. Words like
cancer - stage four - rare and aggressive - no cure - these words
can challenge even the most faithful. Then, of course, we made the
mistake of going on the internet to investigate pancreatic cancer.
That wiped out all but the faintest glimmer of hope.

However, when I made our situation public we were inundated
with assurances of prayer and testimonies of healing. One friend
from Cameroon recorded the miracle of her uncle overcoming
pancreatic cancer in four separate voice messages (they are limited
to about 30 seconds before they cut you off). I can't tell you how
her perseverance to encourage me meant as much as the testimony
she gave. It was invaluable to hear her voice and the assurance with
which she spoke about beating this disease. Did I mention that she's
a doctor? People from all over the world began expressing their
love, sent testimonies, and "pressed like" on the Facebook posts to
let us know they were praying, and we were not alone. I'll never
forget the change in Bert's countenance when he began reading the
responses and seeing how many people were praying for him -
immersed in an ocean of encouragement and faith that restored our
own ability to have hope again.

Some of the most poignant and meaningful were from my

daughter, Sarah. Dealing with her grief at this news, she would still send me reminders of the many miraculous healings we have seen in our family and ministry. "Remember the time Boyd was rushed by ambulance to Valley Children's Hospital with pneumonia and was completely healthy when he arrived at the hospital?" "Remember the time Tessa received miraculously healing from craniosynostosis?" "Remember the time God healed Gram of breast cancer?" These reminders literally injected hope because we had lived and shared these experiences. They felt tangible.

In the first chapter of Joshua, he faced crossing the Jordan River at flood stage to step into God's promised land. Not only was he to lead but he had to do it without Moses, who had been his spiritual father for over 40 years. God spoke to him, "Be strong and courageous." Not once but four times. He was encouraging him, imparting a sense of strength and partnership. Bert and I were facing a river of fear of our own. Our friends became the voice, God, saying you are not alone. You are not orphans; you are not abandoned; you are not without hope. I am with you. We were able to get past our fear and hopelessness because of the encouragement we received.

I am mindful that this is not a one-way street. We all need encouragement from time to time, but it is just as essential to be the encourager. Health requires an outlet for what we receive. The difference between the Red Sea and the Dead Sea is that one has an outlet, and one doesn't. One has life, and one is dead. Please pray and ask God who in your area of influence needs encouragement today. They may not be able to put their need out there as we did, but he can tell you who needs courage even if you don't know the details. Pray for them or send them a text. Try to give them a call. Find a way to communicate to them that they are in your prayers. Impart the gift of courage to someone else today. It only costs a little time, and it could mean everything to them in their time of need.

Prayer Illustration

Father God, Please show me the faces of my friends needing encouragement today. Please remind me of testimonies that will uphold them in their need and remind them of who you are. Please remind me to reach out to them today and be a connection for your grace. In Jesus' name, Amen.

Excerpts from my Facebook timeline:
12/9/16
Dear friends,
Please remember to pray and declare life for my husband Bert today! We choose to believe GODS report which declares life abundant. I do appreciate your words of encouragement. They are feeding his spirit and that is exactly what we need. Any testimonies of healing are especially helpful. Thank you Greg F. Can we connect for prayer soon? Felicia M. can you message me the testimony of healing you referenced yesterday? You would not believe how hopeful Bert became after reading the words from yesterday's post. Sherri L. your testimony completely changed his demeanor! It was life giving!
We utterly reject any word that would teach that God has allowed or caused this assault on his body. Words like that only justify the work of Satan. This is straight from the pit and a design of the enemy and illegal. The strategy the Lord gave me is to encourage you to pray for and heal

every afflicted person you encounter. Help me make the devil pay double for this attack.

God has also told me that each prayer prayed for healing brings us one step closer to complete restoration and restitution. If we don't see healing manifest immediately our prayer hasn't failed. It is a battering ram against the scheme of Satan. Our prayers are powerful and effective.

Thank you, thank you, thank you.

6

It Won't Be Easy

(He's Just Being Honest)

And we know that in all things God works for the good of those
who love him, who have been called according to his purpose.
Romans 8:28

When God initially told me our fight wouldn't be easy, I didn't
question it. I was desperate for a plan of action and didn't entirely
absorb what he had said. "It won't be easy." Those words came back
to me in the weeks to come. For a while, I would see them in my
mind and think, "I'm not going near them. I'm not going to consider
that right now." But they would sneak up on me, tap me on the
shoulder and whisper in my ear, "It won't be easy." Why was I
avoiding that thought? Because everything in me believed it should
be easy. I was teetering on the edge of defeat and despair because
it wasn't easy.

Why couldn't it be easy? Why, when we had seen cancer healed,
sight restored, miraculous healings, signs, and wonders, couldn't
this one be easy? Bert had faith. I had faith. We believed in the
authority and power of the believer, casting out demons to see
people set free in unbelievable ways. The vision statement of our
church was to be a resource for God's healing in our region. Yet
here we were, in a fight for his life, and God Himself had declared
it would not be easy.

I didn't trust myself to talk to the Lord about my feelings. I was
so cautious about allowing fear or doubt to rest upon me; I avoided
any thought that might be used by the devil to find a foothold.
Every time it came up, I would say to myself. "Stop it. Don't think

about that. Just believe." But Father God isn't looking for blind faith. He's looking for a faith that he can inform, so it kept coming up until finally, I asked, "Why can't it be easy?" His response was immediate. Scripture flooded my mind. Jesus told his followers they would be persecuted, ostracized, and banished from their own families. They would be tortured and put to death. To quote Paul describing his experiences, "Three times I was beaten with rods, once I was stoned, three times I was shipwrecked, I spent a night and a day in the open sea, I have been constantly on the move. I have been in danger from rivers, in danger from bandits, in danger from my own countrymen, in danger from Gentiles; in danger in the city, in danger in the country, in danger at sea; and in danger from false brothers. I have labored and toiled and have often gone without sleep; I have known hunger and thirst and have often gone without food; I have been cold and naked. Besides everything else, I face daily the pressure of my concern for all the churches." 2 Corinthians 11:25-28 Yet, these were men whose shadows and cast off aprons healed the sick, who raised the dead to life, and who converted thousands and thousands of people in their lifetimes. They stepped into that call knowing full well that it would not be effortless. God had given them the gift of choice. If you choose to follow me and bring my kingdom to earth, it will not be easy, but I will be with you through it.

He reminded me that my faith is not a promise of ease or comfort but a promise of presence. He said, "I'm honest with you. I don't want you to become disillusioned by the severity of this trial. You are facing an enemy who's determined to destroy Bert and - with him - your way of life, your faith, your voice. Overcoming won't be easy, but it is possible. I haven't caused this, but if you will dig in and determine to not give up, I will use it to further my kingdom." I could see how Bert's testimony would impact the world for God's kingdom.

Kingdom Perspective. It's incredible how that perspective strengthened me. How the words I avoided for weeks now increased my faith rather than diminish it. It may sound funny, but I was proud that God trusted me enough to be honest with me (as if he would ever not be). He thought I could "handle the truth."

Kingdom Purpose. I've often heard it said that when your pain has a purpose, it becomes endurable. Just suffering is unbearable, but suffering for a cause gives one strength to see it through. Who would ever go through the pain of childbirth without the promise of a baby? I remember telling myself in the middle of labor, "You're not going to die. Other women have done this for centuries and lived. This pain will pass, and you will have a baby at the end of it." It didn't alleviate my pain, but it did remind me that there was a purpose to it.

Indeed, Christianity is no promise of blue skies and sunshine. If it were, evangelism would be so easy! We are not promised easy; we are promised presence. To be honest, not all hardship is a result of our kingdom endeavors. Sometimes it is merely the law of reaping and sowing. Sometimes, it's the result of living in a sin-broken world. Whatever the cause, if we invite God into the circumstances, he can give every trial meaning. He can turn the weapons meant for our destruction back against the destroyer. He can bring good out of the darkest hour. If we invite him to, he will.

Take time this week as you pray. Invite God for His perspective on some of the things you've faced or are facing. Ask him to reveal what use your hard time could serve and where he was or where he is in the storm. Get some perspective, take hold of his purpose and hang in there.

Prayer Illustration

Heavenly Father, Things look pretty bleak from where I am. I need a different perspective. I need to see things through your eyes. Do my circumstances have any purpose? Can any good come from these things? I know you can redeem anything if I trust you with it, so I place this situation in your hands and ask that you give me your view in the meantime. In Jesus' name, Amen.

Excerpt from my Facebook timeline:

2/5/19

Daily prayer reminder

Bert Boyd says I'm grouchy. This is after getting 4 hours of sleep 15 minutes at a time because he could not get comfortable. We made the rounds from our bed to his recliner to the hospital bed to the couch then back to our bed, etc. I'm not grouchy, I'm a saint.

Thank you for remembering us in your prayers. Probably saved his life in more ways than one!

Please press like when you have prayed.

#prayforBert #prayersmatter #godisgood #winning #hejustfeelslikecrap #ididntkillhim #hegottosleepallday

7

Payback

"Now, Lord, consider their threats and enable your servants to
speak your word with great boldness. Stretch out your hand to
heal and perform miraculous signs and wonders
through the name of your holy servant Jesus."
After they prayed, the place where they were meeting was
shaken. And they were all filled with the Holy Spirit and spoke
the word of God boldly. Acts 4:29-31

One of the most recurrent themes the devil has tried to play in my
head goes something like this: "You call yourself a healer? Why
can't you heal your husband?" Another theme would be, "No one
will ever come to a healing church whose Senior Leader has
cancer." Or "You may as well stop praying for others. You have lost
all credibility." Finally, the ever-popular "If it's always God's will
to heal, why hasn't Bert been healed. You are deceived." Truth be
told, at an earlier stage in my life, that voice would have undone me.
However, I've had 20 years of partnering with God for healing. I
knew it was always his will to heal. I also recognized the strategy
behind the voice. If we quit believing for and praying with people
for healing, the more significant battle was lost. We weren't
fighting just for Bert's miracle but for our church to move forward
into its destiny as a place of healing.

In response to the barrage of accusations from the devil, God
gave me a counter-strategy. Make him pay. Go on the attack and
pray for every person that looks like they are in pain. Instead of
backing off, get bolder. Risk more. And so I challenged my church
to start a campaign of praying for strangers. We used the

introduction, "Excuse me. My church has challenged me to pray for anyone I see in pain, and I noticed you appeared to be experiencing pain. Would it be OK to pray for you?" I would use that introductory phrase quite often, even though I was the person who had done the challenging.

I would love to say that I went after every person I saw in need, but I can't. Sometimes I would talk myself right out of faith, making excuses to avoid approaching a stranger. But not every time and it seemed the more I risked, the easier it got to pray and see results.

Step out in the area where you find yourself under a specific attack. We call this operating in the opposite spirit. For instance, if you are always broke, try performing an act of generosity. If you experience frequent illness, pray for someone else to be healed. If you find yourself overlooked or disrespected, go out of your way to show honor to someone else. Remember, the devil always attacks the potential destiny he is most afraid of. If he has the slightest hint of what God has called you to, he will move to destroy it, which explains Pharaoh's slaughter of the Hebrew babies in Moses' day and Herod's slaughter of the children in Bethlehem.

Prayer Illustration

Lord, Please help me discern between your voice and the voice of the deceiver. Help me to remember that you created me with a destiny and that failures are just teachable moments. I want to live out your plan for me, not the counterplan of the devil. Please give me the courage to overcome my fear and pursue your purpose for me. In Jesus' name, Amen.

Excerpts from my Facebook timeline:

12/12/16

Monday morning! Thank you for praying for my husband, Bert, today! Your prayers are propelling us toward victory over this illness. Please pray specifically for favor with medical people as we seek to secure a biopsy and direction as to what steps we should be taking next.

I have determined to pray for anyone I encounter that appears to be ill or in pain. I stopped a woman at Walmart who was in pain and she told me she had cancer through out her body! After prayer both she and her husband were greatly encouraged and I know I dealt a blow to the devil with my prayer! Please consider joining me in this determination. Let's make the enemy pay for touching the children of God!

Please press the like button when you pray. It so encouraging to know you are standing with us. Much love friends!

12/23/16

Daily Prayer reminder

This is the second time I've typed this. The first went out to FB ozone. Sorry if it reposts. Yesterday at Starbucks Audrey and I got to pray with a girl on crutches with her ankle wrapped. After a brief prayer for healing I told her check it out. The look on her face was priceless as she was able to increasingly move her foot and ankle without pain.

Take that devil! That's another one for Bert! Audrey says "We have to go to Starbucks more often! " lol. As good as the ER.

Thank you thank you thank you. Not just for praying for Bert but for making the devil pay! Every prayer increases the kingdom and deals a blow to the enemy.

Please press like when you have prayed and feel free to share with your friends.

#Prayforbert #winning #godisgood #prayersmatter #ihatethedevil #makeempay

04/09/17

Daily prayer reminder

Palm Sunday! Hosanna!

Yesterday we went in to Kona and stopped at a little street fair with vendors and live music and dancers. I was led by the spirit to one booth of hand made jewelry. Chatting with the proprietor, she shared how and why she started making jewelry. I felt that I was to honor her and her work was lovely so I bought several pieces (one of which she spontaneously gave me). After the purchase I asked if I could pray And bless her business. As I was praying, she began to cry pretty hard. When I finished, she said "can I tell you something? I may have cancer." So, of course I prayed again. Yeeeeeessss! When I left her both she and her family were all smiles.

How good is God? We almost didn't stop there. It wasn't convenient. But God . . . What a blessing for me to pass on what you have been so generous with. The prayer of a righteous person is worth more then gold.

Thank you thank you thank you! Please press like when you have prayed and feel free to share with praying friends.

#prayforBert #godisgood #prayersmatter #winning #scoreoneforteamjesus #prayitforward #handmadejewelryisthebomb #prayersaremorepreciousthangold #butmakeapurchasetoo #dontbecheap

8
Seek and You Will Find

Jesus answered: "Don't you know me, Philip, even after I have
been among you such a long time? Anyone who has seen me has
seen the Father. How can you say, 'Show us the Father'?
Don't you believe that I am in the Father, and that the Father is
in me? The words I say to you are not just my own.
Rather, it is the Father, living in me, who is doing his work.
Believe me when I say that I am in the Father and the Father is in
me; or at least believe on the evidence of the miracles themselves.
John 14:9-11

What do you believe about God? I have a little saying that goes
like this, "You get what you expect." In other words, your brain will
look for confirmation of what you already believe. It's called
confirmation bias. If you think no one likes you, your brain will
ignore every friendly overture and focus on the one person who
failed to talk to you at a party. If you believe you're destined to fail,
your brain will latch onto the mistakes you make at work and write
off any successful endeavors as luck, not skill. Many people say, "I'll
believe it when I see it." However, what happens is that we only see
what we already believe! Despite what you may think, our brains do
not provide us with analytical, unbiased information to be processed
into informed ideas and decisions. Our minds work very hard to
substantiate whatever we already believe to be true. Our emotional
truth will always take the lead over our intellectual truth.
Confirmation bias can be a blessing or a curse depending on what
you believe to be true. For us, this dynamic is the blessing that got
us through the worst days of our battle.

Because we were already grounded in the belief that God is good, we saw his goodness everywhere. From the beginning, we were very intentional in looking for and sharing the ways we were seeing God's goodness each day. The doors that opened to get into the right doctors, the appointments that came through, even the benign cyst that had brought the tumors to light were evidence that God was for us not against us. That core belief fed our hope and faith for a miracle when we could have easily despaired. We wanted to testify in a way that encouraged those that were contending for us. Many of our friends began to see God in a new light. They, too, began to believe that he wasn't the author of their troubles but the source of their strength.

It helped we believed in and embraced a theology of his goodness and mercy before we experienced the crisis of this attack. I won't write a thesis on this viewpoint except to say, when you read the Gospels in the Bible, you can clearly see the heart of God revealed in the person of his son, Jesus. Jesus, who healed, fed, delivered, and restored people. Jesus, who calmed storms and wept at the grief of his friends. Jesus, who died for our sake. Knowing a good and loving God got us through the hardest times and inspired us to share with the world, at every opportunity, where and when we saw his goodness.

What do you believe about God? I have good news for you, God is good. God is not angry with you. He is not waiting to punish your shortcomings or shame you. God is not distant and aloof. He does not cause sickness. He destroys it. He has not caused your misery to make you a better person or teach you a lesson. What do you believe about God? I have more good news for you; you can change your mind. It takes directed, intentional effort, but you can do it. Start by declaring your new way of thinking out loud. Hearing is believing. Ask yourself throughout the day, "If I had to prove God is good, what in this situation would I use?" Take the time to read some of the miracles included in the Gospels, and as you read them, replace the name Jesus with the words "Father God." Jesus is not the hero protecting us from Father God, the bad guy. Jesus repeatedly emphasized that he and the Father are one. One mind. One heart.

Prayer Illustration

Father God, Show me what lies I believe about your goodness. (Pause and listen for his response.) What is your truth about that lie? (Again, look for his response.) What action do you want me to take to dismantle that lie? (Listen.) In Jesus' name, Amen.

Excerpts from my Facebook timeline:
12/17/16
Daily Prayer reminder. Saturday. Haha. I wrote that and spell check changed it to saturated. That is what we have been. Saturated with love and prayers from all of you. Thank you thank you thank you. You can't possibly know how it has helped.
Yesterday was the third of many miracles. We are scheduled for an endoscopic biopsy the first week of January. Our oncologist gave us no hope to get in to this doctor and our gastroenterologist a slim hope but God . . .

The first miracle is that our gastroenterologist and his staff are all Christian and we all prayed together after our consult. He said "we have seen miracles in this office. "
The second is that we were received into the oncologists office within a

week of the CT scan. He told us that they have 15 applications a week and can only take about 5. He was surprised that his nurse had wrangled us in (which she did the day before taking an 8 week sick leave.)

I know this is a long post but I want you to know that your prayers are like bulldozers making a way for God against the designs of the enemy! Your prayers matter and they are carrying us through this with grace. Please don't stop!

Of course, we are looking forward to the ultimate miracle - healing.

Please press like when you have prayed. Feel free to share with your friends. #Prayforbert #winning #godisgood #prayersmatter

12/22/16

Daily Prayer reminder

Thank you for your prayers! We spent a good part of the day in medical offices yesterday and I must confess the atmosphere is not conducive to increased Faith.

Oh but God! On the way home, I received such a strong word of encouragement from our dear friend Ken in which we were reminded that we are not fighting this alone. That the faith of our friends is filling in where ours gaps.

Then I came home to find most of my presents wrapped by Sarah and Audrey! Almost as if God was saying - you do what you have to, I will provide for what you can't do.

Thank you dear friends for pouring out Faith where ours is thin. For covering us and believing with us that miracles are a way of life in the kingdom.

Thank you thank you thank you! Please press like when you have prayed for Bert's healing. Feel free to share.

#Prayforbert #winning #godisgood #prayersmatter #ihatethedevil #mydaughtersrock

12/26/16

Daily Prayer reminder

I hope that your Christmas was everything you hoped it would be! We started the day with our family tradition of reading the Christmas Story with cinnamon rolls on the side. Such a great reminder that putting the kingdom first doesn't mean you can't enjoy it.

Today I am reminded that the cornerstone of our faith is based on God's goodness not on suffering. Only a good and loving God would choose to step out of eternity to endure the confines of humanity. Only love could drive God into the Manger and ultimately to the cross.

That kind of love is triumphant over the works of the devil in all its forms. Even disease.

Thank you for agreeing with me today that it is the will of a good and loving God to heal Bert. Your prayers are the instruments that God is using to see his will fulfilled!

Thank you thank you thank you!

Please press like when you have prayed and feel free to share with your friends.

#Prayforbert #godisgood #prayersmatter #winning #yourwillbedoneyourkingdomcome #ihatethedevil

9
I Would like to Exchange This Please

"And everyone who has left houses or brothers or sisters or father or mother or children or fields for my sake will receive a hundred times as much and will inherit eternal life." Matthew 19:29

Anyone who is going through a trial or crisis will have moments when emotion overwhelms the most faithful. Let's face it; even Jesus prayed the cup to be taken from him in the Garden of Gethsemane. Whether it is directly from the circumstances of the trial or something completely unrelated, we are more prone to experience anger, fear, disappointment, unforgiveness, or grief. Our response may be directed at the circumstances, yourself, others in the situation, or even God. Rest assured, those moments will come - often quietly, secretly, and unsuspected. Although it is typical and expected to experience these feelings, it is toxic to allow them to find a resting place in our thoughts. The danger is not in having the thought or feeling; it is in allowing it to become entrenched in your thought life. In other words, it's normal to feel angry but exhausting to stay angry. It's normal to feel disappointed but crushing to become hopeless. When we embrace our negative emotions as the barometer of what is right, our perspectives shift and become skewed. They become the filter through which we view and relate to God during our crisis. When we need him most, we allow these feelings to become walls or barriers between our heavenly Father and us. And God will not violate our walls even if it's for our good.

As Bert and I were going through this process, I would find myself feeling all these feelings and more. I would love to pretend that I never had a bad day, never accused God, never despaired, but I would be a liar. I often shared some struggles publicly, but really what I shared was usually just the tip of an iceberg of being overwhelmed. Early on, I developed a discipline of asking the Lord to reveal anything that had come between us during my soaking/prayer time. I was often prompted to do so because I was having a hard time connecting with Him. I felt he was distant. Sure enough, he would bring up something I was angry about, someone who had offended me, or an area of worry and fear. That is when I would (and still do) practice the spiritual discipline of the exchange.

The "exchange." Many of us are familiar with this spiritual principle because of the transaction at the cross. The cross is where we exchanged our sinfulness for his righteousness. If you study the life of Jesus you find that whatever you give him, good or bad, he gives you something better in exchange. And so I would take whatever he showed me (fear, doubt, unforgiveness), confess and repent of any sin attached to it, ask him to take it from me, and inquire as to what he had in exchange for me. What a blessing to hear the things he was blessing me with each morning we met. Peace in place of rage, hope in place of fear, healing for unforgiveness. And he is faithful every time, no matter how often I show up with my weaknesses. It may sound funny, but it's kind of like a trip to the dry cleaners, you show up with stained, wrinkled, and smelly stuff. In exchange, you get clean, pressed, and fresh stuff back. Every time. No shame or guilt, just good.

I encourage you to take a few moments and invite Jesus to reveal any thought, attitude, or action that is hindering you from drawing near to him. When I do this, I will often receive snapshots of the previous days surface with negative feelings and experiences attached. If you find this is also your experience, practice the dynamic of the exchange with him.

Prayer Illustration

Lord, Please show me if I've allowed anything to come between us. I confess I am disappointed about (fill in the blank.) I repent of my lack of hope and ask you to forgive me. Please take this disappointment from me. What do you have in exchange?" (He will always give better than he receives.) In Jesus' name, Amen.

Excerpt from my Facebook timeline:

12/28/16

Daily Prayer reminder

Thank you for praying for Bert's healing today. We had a rough night.

I am reminded of the spiritual dynamic of exchange. I have been using it quite a bit these days. "Lord, I give you my fear/anger/ unforgiveness /etc., what do you give me in exchange? And God's so good, he always gives better than he gets.

What is amazing to me is that I have been able to recognize when I'm worried, etc. That it has not been able to sneak up on me with little cat feet and settle in to become a stronghold. That isn't because I'm so spiritually sensitive but because I am surrounded by the prayers of the saints. You have given me the strength to lean into power of the exchange.

Come to me all who are weary and heavy laden and I will give you rest . . for my yoke is easy and my burden is light.

Thank you thank you thank you. Your prayers are strength and life and light in the darkness!

Please press like when you have prayed and feel free to share. Bert and I appreciate you!

#Prayforbert #prayersmatter #godisgood #winning #exchange #ihatethedevil

10
Don't Give an Inch

For our struggle is not against flesh and blood, but against the rulers, against the authorities, against the powers of this dark world and against the spiritual forces of evil in the heavenly realms. Therefore put on the full armor of God, so that when the day of evil comes, you may be able to stand your ground, and after you have done everything, to stand. Ephesians 6:12-13

I surrendered my life to Jesus as an adult in a United Methodist church at the age of 33. I'd experienced a few churches, false religions, and even a cult in the years prior, but nothing ever stuck. So it was as an adult that I came to salvation at the Visalia United Methodist Church in Visalia, California. The beauty of the Methodist church is they are very tolerant of numerous religious traditions. These include extreme liberalism, evangelicalism, fundamentalism, and even charismatic or pentecostal proponents. You could find both cessationists and word of faith believers worshiping next to each other in this particular church. Everything coming from the leadership was very moderate and carefully inoffensive, but there were undercurrents of varying traditions flowing throughout the church that were tolerated and sometimes celebrated. It was here that I was drawn to the gifts and working of the Holy Spirit and where I discovered the power of prayer.

Many people I connected with during my time on staff there had come out of a charismatic/pentecostal tradition. Most of them were significantly older than me, becoming true spiritual mothers and fathers of the faith. They introduced me to the United Methodist Holy Spirit conferences, the gift of praying in a prayer language and other ideas such as impartation through the laying on of hands, fasting, and healing prayer. That is how I came to be included in an exercise that increased my understanding of spiritual warfare, the despicable and evil nature of the devil, and the significance of persevering by faith as God's strength is made available to me.

Early in my faith life, I participated in a prayer movement for the period of Lent. We decided to pray for the finances of the families within our church. Our church was in the middle of a transition from our old building to building a new one, and money was tight. The idea behind this prayer movement was if our families saw a breakthrough in their finances, so would the church. There were twelve of us, so we took the church directory and divided the pages between us.

I've never been a travailing kind of prayer warrior. I kept my prayer to a pretty simple "Lord please bless the finances of these families" and would then read out each of the family names listed on my set of pages. On the face of it, I must say in comparison to my more spiritual (and long-winded) friends, I felt like my particular families had gotten the short end of the stick.

Shortly after we began this exercise, my youngest son, Anthony, started experiencing seizures out of the blue. He was in fourth grade and had never given any indication that he may have epilepsy. We belonged to a form of insurance that hindered us from reaching appropriate pediatric specialists right away, and it was a terrifying and traumatic episode for our entire family. Still, in addition to beseeching God to heal my son, every night, I would obediently pray for the finances of my Methodist families. It was then that I would hear this still small voice whisper, "If you stop praying for these people, the seizures will stop." I can remember the first time I listened to that whisper. I thought I was making it up myself or imagining it. But it persisted and would come every night as I prayed, "Please bless the finances of these families." I asked God if it were possibly true that my simple unremarkable prayers were actually instigating this assault on my son's body and possibly his brain. "Yes," he responded. "The attack is meant to keep you from completing your assignment." I can honestly say I've never been so tempted to quit anything like I was at that time. I was anguished for my son and didn't feel much of a connection with the people for whom I was praying. I knew them, but I did not love them like I loved my child. I went back to the Lord and asked, "What will happen if I quit praying." He showed me a picture of a map with green and black areas. The green spaces were being consumed by the black spaces like a light being snuffed out. I heard the Lord say, "If you give an inch now, you will NEVER stop giving ground. Any being that would attack an innocent child and make him suffer will never be satisfied no matter what you sacrifice to him. Don't quit."

I did not quit. I prayed through Lent, and Anthony had his last seizure on Good Friday. There were physical and emotional ramifications that he suffered, mainly due to the medications prescribed to him. But he's overcome them and never again has he experienced a seizure. One of the families I had prayed for shared with me that they had never had such a successful year, and others shared testimonies of money unlooked for or sales and commissions. The church finances saw a breakthrough. It seems my prayers were far more critical than I understood.

I learned some hard lessons that year. I learned the devil is more despicable than I imagined. I learned that quitting is not quitting, it's retreating, and I learned that even the simplest prayer is powerful. I learned that we are in a war where there is no neutral ground, no demilitarized zone, and the enemy considers everything fair game. I learned that nothing would satisfy the hatred of the devil except the annihilation of everything good. I learned there is no compromise because the devil hates all of humanity, those who resist him and those who partner with him.

Throughout our battle, occasionally I would hear a still small voice whisper, "You should close the church. Stay home with your husband. Enjoy the time you have before it's too late." This persistent devil is also a consistent devil, and I've heard that voice before.

Take some time to invite the Lord to reveal any area of compromise or temptation for it in your life. Resolve to shake it off, get up, and move ahead. It's never too late to re-engage in the fight. Ask him to show you the map of where you have taken ground for his kingdom. Be encouraged and know that sometimes just standing your ground is a victory.

Prayer Illustration

Heavenly Father, Please make me aware of any area in my life that I've compromised because of the devil. Please give me a plan to overcome in these areas and help me take back any ground I've given away. Please help me to stand firm as I resist this enemy! In Jesus' name, Amen.

Excerpts from my Facebook timeline:

12/20/16

Daily Prayer reminder

As I woke up this morning God reminded me of a time when I first began to partner with him in prayer for others.

The devil immediately tried to stop me by assaulting my youngest son with seizures. Every night, I would go to pray for families in our church and I would hear "if you stop praying, the seizures will stop. " The temptation to give in was overwhelming and very real. But the Lord showed me that I was at a cross roads. If I gave an inch, satan would never stop taking ground from me. I resolved to continue praying and the seizures stopped. Since then I have participated in miracles, healing and the salvation of hundreds of people.

The Lord reminded me of this morning. I believe that the ministry that Bert and I have been birthing is about to explode forth. And the devil is trying to abort it in the third trimester.

But I say no. No I will not ever give an inch. The abortionist is a liar and in the kingdom abortion is illegal.

You are praying for much more than one man's victory over cancer. Thank you thank you thank you.

Please press like when you have prayed. Feel free to share with your friends.

#Prayforbert #winning #godisgood #prayersmatter #nevergiveupneversurrender #ihatethedevil

02/01/17

Daily Prayer reminder

Good is amazing! Yesterday Audrey and I prayed for God to help us see people who needed prayer. After school she told me she had prayed for 3 boys at school with leg injuries and that 2 of the 3 received a measure of healing. (She didn't have time to follow up with #3).

God told me we needed to make the devil pay for this attack and we are going after it. The only person I saw in pain was in such a rush, I couldn't get her attention to offer prayer. Give me eyes to see Lord!

Thank you for your partnership! Bert is better today than yesterday and trying to make up for lost calories. We are so thankful for you, our doctors, family and of course God!

Please press like when you have prayed and feel free to share with praying friends.

#Prayforbert #godisgood #prayersmatter #winning #makeempay #thatsmygirl

11
Character Matters

And do not grieve the Holy Spirit of God, with whom you were
sealed for the day of redemption. Ephesians 4:30

The first chapter of Ephesians states that we have been sealed in
Jesus by the Holy Spirit. The same Spirit who raised Jesus from the
dead is the seal that guarantees our access to the inheritance of all
that Jesus made available to us. It was with this in mind when I
asked the Father, "Lord if I have access to the same Spirit that
rested upon Jesus, why can't I just speak a word and heal Bert?" It
was a sincere question not borne of grief but a genuine desire to
understand. His response was immediate.

"Nancy," he responded. "How many times a day do you think
Jesus cussed?"

I should explain at this point that cussing has been an ongoing
struggle for me. Growing up in the "hood," everyone I knew used
language that could make a sailor blush. It was only natural to
drop the f* bomb when you stubbed your toe, lost your temper, or
just wanted to emphasize a point in the conversation. When I
surrendered my heart to Jesus, I gave up cussing for the most part
recognizing it as "unwholesome talk." I didn't want my behavior to
be a stumbling block to the people I encountered. However, I would
find that in situations of extreme stress or unguarded conversation,
I would revert right back to the language of my youth. It has been
an ongoing struggle.

His question set in motion a video in my mind of the many times
during the week I'd not only cussed but partnered with sin in other
ways. Anger, judgmentalism, evil thoughts, etc., you get the

picture. He didn't reduce me in shame but made me aware of how often I had allowed sin to find a place in my mind.

Again he asked, "How many times a day did Jesus cuss?"

"I'm pretty sure Jesus didn't cuss," I replied.

"That's right," he said. "If you want to increase in power, you must increase in holiness."

I was dumbstruck. The reality of what God was saying sank in. I already knew that holiness increased the anointing of the Holy Spirit, but now I KNEW it did. I've rarely been so sure of something or so convicted. I could see a myriad of ways that I had tolerated or, worse yet, justified sin.

We don't need to pursue holiness for our salvation since we are made righteous by the cross and set free from the covenant of performance. However, if we expect to host heaven, we can't act like hell. Since God will never partner with sin, the pursuit of holiness dramatically increases our capacity to carry God's Spirit. The less sin, the greater freedom he has to flow through you.

For some, just being saved will be enough. Going to church consistently, being good parents and moral citizens, having empathy for the suffering, and being charitable will be the highlight of their life. I honestly believe, except for going to church, any atheist or agnostic could do the same. Morality, kindness, and charity are essential, but they are not what sets Christians apart. It is the height of arrogance to believe that we have a monopoly on human decency. These things are not what Jesus came to set in motion. He came to release the kingdom of God on earth. There is a responsibility that comes with our salvation. First, to partner with him to destroy the works of the devil. Second, to bring the atmosphere of heaven to earth. We must live in a way that hosts more of the Holy Spirit that we might release an encounter with God's presence.

I want to say that I've left behind the multitude of little sins that slip past me every day, but I can't. I do believe that this conversation with him made me much more aware of my "slips" but I have a ways to go yet. The good news is that there is actually something you and I can do to increase our ability to carry God's kingdom forward - to change the world. Resist temptation. Don't tolerate old habits. Change the way you think. When you fail, get up and start again. Pursue holiness.

Prayer Illustration

Lord, I want to grow in my effectiveness at increasing your kingdom. I also want to experience heightened intimacy with you. Please make me more aware of sin and potential sin throughout my day, so I resist it's bait. I already know that my salvation is secure, but I long to experience your presence at higher levels here on earth. Show me ways to defeat old habits and break out of my "mind ruts." In Jesus' name, Amen.

Excerpt from my Facebook timeline:

03/03/17

Daily Prayer reminder

One of the things this experience has produced in me is a greater desire to passionately pursue holiness. Not as a performance issue but as a desire to grow in intimate knowledge and understanding of my inheritance as a daughter of God.

More than ever, I have come to utterly hate disease. I see it as a tool of the enemy for death and destruction in so many ways and I burn with the desire to eradicate it. It doesn't just kill the body, it destroys joy and spreads misery. If I want to walk in the power and authority that Jesus purchased for me, then I must consistently choose the holiness he makes available to me. When it comes to releasing heaven, I am often my own greatest hindrance.

Thank goodness for your prayers! Together we are making the devil miserable hahahahaha!

Please press like when you have prayed and feel free to share with praying friends.

#Prayforbert #godisgood #prayersmatter #winning #quitcussingalready #holinesscarriesheaveninitsshadow #johnglakeannointing

12
Why Jesus Suffered

Surely he took up our infirmities and carried our sorrows, yet we considered him stricken by God, smitten by him, and afflicted. But he was pierced for our transgressions, he was crushed for our iniquities; the punishment that brought us peace was upon him, and by his wounds we are healed. Isaiah 53:4-5

I've always valued faith with understanding over blind faith. I may be too intellectual, but I've never been able to ascribe to the "I believe, I believe, I believe" mentality that I've witnessed in some. I don't mean any disparagement, simply that I am wired differently. Sometimes face value isn't enough for me, and I need to understand. Much like Mary asking, "How will this be since I am a virgin?" I've often found myself with questions of "why" and "how" as I've navigated this river of faith that carries me forward. I've found once I understand something, I own it for life.

In the healing ministry, the first Bible verses you learn are from Isaiah 53:4-5. To paraphrase, "He has carried our sickness and pain, and by his scourging, we are healed." I've quoted some form of this many times as encouragement that disease, sickness, and affliction are illegal because Jesus suffered. "By his stripes, we are healed." If you ever have the privilege of praying with a bunch of healing ministers, you will hear that phrase quite often. I have believed these words to be true. Jesus suffered "pre-cross" to overcome disease in the world. That was the purpose of his suffering the indignity and pain of the torment. Our sins were paid ON the cross, our diseases BEFORE the cross. After all, what perfect lamb was tortured and whipped before its sacrifice on the altar? His enduring that suffering was why we no longer had to.

I did not doubt the veracity of that statement. Yet, as I quoted that scripture while praying in the early morning, I found myself questioning God. How? How did Jesus suffering the brutality of the whip, become healing for us? If I were going to hang Bert's life on scripture, I needed to understand more.

One of the most remarkable things about an honest conversation with God is that he isn't intimidated by our questions. His response was gentle and straightforward.

"Nancy, you realize I couldn't get sick."

That was all. It took me a moment, but I got it. Jesus couldn't carry a literal disease because every leper he touched was healed! No cancer, no flu, not even a cold, could find a place in him. Instead, he submitted to the abasement that sickness creates within us and the physical devastation it visits upon us. His suffering represented all that illness does to our bodies and souls in graphic detail. The torment of his accusers illustrates how the devil uses sickness to torment the world. The humiliating antagonism of his captors perfectly illustrates the demonic delight of every afflicting demon and strong man of disease at the degradation of humanity.

This conversation resulted in two things happening within me. First, more than ever before, I knew that the disease attacking Bert was demonic and illegal. Second, I saw sickness for the weapon of the devil that it was and hated it. I realized blaming God for any illness anywhere was to blaspheme the Holy Spirit - to blame him for the works of the devil.

Take some time and re-read in the gospels the account of Jesus' arrest, trial, and crucifixion. Invite God to reveal to you how each indignity and brutality is a type for the effects of disease and sickness upon humanity. Then ask him to uncover any area in your life that you have accommodated the thought that God caused illness in someone's life. If he shows you that you have harbored these thoughts, confess it, and ask for help to repent. He is quick to forgive and faithful to renew.

Prayer Illustration

Father God, I believe your word. I believe you suffered indignity, torment, and pain so that we would have victory over disease and sickness. Please show me when I have not accepted your word that I might confess your truth and repent. I know you are faithful to forgive and restore, so I thank you for it now. In Jesus' name, Amen.

Excerpt from my Facebook timeline:

02/05/2017

Daily Prayer reminder

Bert is so good today! He received so much Prayer this week, you can see it physically reflected in his being.

When Jesus bore our infirmities he chose to illustrate it by allowing violence and degradation to be done to his body. It is such a graphic illustration of what the devil is doing to us when he perpetrates illness and disease within us. Our hearts burn within us when we consider the injustice of His suffering.

In the same way, in the spirit, healing is a violent area of warfare in which we respond to our foe like for like. Every gentle healing prayer that is prayed by sweet and tender hearts is an act of violence against a voracious and insidious monster assigned to hinder, cripple and kill the beloved of God. When we partner with God for healing, we declare our value and appreciation for the price paid for that healing and we strike a blow to the one who would invalidate God's sacrifice.

Thank you for partnering with us for healing today. You are the champions of God and your prayers make the devil tremble.

Please press like when you have prayed and feel free to share with friends who pray.

#Prayforbert #godisgood #prayersmatter #winning #onceforall #byhisstripeswearehealed #fanaticsrock

13

Speaking Peace to the Chaos

"You of little faith," Jesus replied, "why are you so afraid?"
Then He got up and rebuked the winds and the sea, and it was
perfectly calm." Matthew 8:26

Pastor Bill Johnson of Bethel Church in Redding, California, has a fantastic teaching on Jesus having authority over the storm. He teaches that Jesus had power over the storm because, unlike his disciples, he was able to sleep in the midst of it. The bottom line is that we have authority over anything we have peace over. This teaching is excellent except for one thing - this storm scared the bleep out of me right from the start!

Cancer is the uncontrolled growth of abnormal cells in the body. It not only disrupts your cells, but it also disrupts your whole world. The word "cancer" creates fear in nearly every heart. Add the words "stage four," and the fear is intensified. Your heart pounds, your mind races, and you experience this sinking feeling of hopelessness in the pit of your stomach. When the news becomes public, you are deluged with "cures" from well-meaning friends that have heard of countless remedies that our medical society has chosen to overlook. You find yourself grasping at every straw of hope that is offered because you are not in control over what is happening to you or the person you love. In short, cancer creates chaos.

When I initially asked God how to pray against cancer, he responded, "Release peace." I didn't have peace to release and had to trust it was there in spite of my feelings. I reminded myself that God is not your emotions and spoke peace over Bert's pancreas and liver.   At a conference in Redding, I was affirmed in my prayer strategy when we approached Chris Gore, Director of the Healing Ministries at Bethel, for prayer.   The first thing he prayed was, "I release peace and rebuke the chaos of cancer." Bert said, his insides were jumping around going crazy as Chris approached him.   The demonic reacting to the healing authority that Chris carries.

Before that encounter, I found the atmosphere around us was changing as we learned to rely on the body of Christ for support. The prayers of our friends created fertile ground for peace to take root. Each day of life was a victory that increased our expectations for ultimate success.

One of the most significant ways I was able to increase my own peace was to face the worst possible outcome full on. During prayer one morning, I asked myself the question, "What if Bert does not live through this?" As I faced this fear, each scenario of tragedy presented itself, and God responded, "I will take care of that." Instead of running from my fear, I faced it, and God reminded me of how he had been with me in the past and would not abandon me in the future. I felt fear dissolve as peace for the future settled on me like a blanket.

Prayer Illustration

Heavenly Father, Please help me to identify the storms of my life. What is my peace level? Please give me a prayer strategy to raise it. Show me who I can invite to contend with me against this storm. (Ask God the big "What If" questions. Bring your fears out into the light and allow him to respond to them.) Thank you that your help is just a prayer away. In Jesus' name, Amen.

Excerpt from my Facebook timeline:

02/03

Daily Prayer reminder

Watching Bert rest this morning I am impressed with how easy it has become to sleep in the midst of this storm. Our confidence in God's victory grows stronger each day. Waiting on God's miracle could become discouraging but we are far from discouraged. Instead it feels like waiting for a package in the mail. You are anxious for it to arrive but there is no doubt that it's coming. The order has been paid for (including shipping and tax) and we are confident in the delivery system.

Rather, it's the little things that tend to undo us. Painful blisters, bad traffic, missing toiletries. These are the things that tend to disrupt our peace. Silly isn't it? Cancer - no problem. Forgotten dental floss- argh!

When Bert broke out in blisters in his mouth it was almost unbearable. We scoured the drug store for anything that would provide relief. Of course he was so distracted, he didn't eat or drink and really lost ground. Imagine our chagrin after 4 days of misery when his doctor said "I wish you had called me right away. We have medicine for that." Medicine that provided immediate relief and began the healing process. It didn't occur to us that the doctor that heals cancer also treats mouth sores.

Through this process we are learning to pull EVERY situation into the kingdom. God cares about the little things as much as the big ones because it's the little things that wear you down and steal your peace.

Thank you for your prayers! They are equipping us to sleep through this storm and as Bill Johnson says, "you have authority over the storms you can sleep through."

Please press like When you have prayed and feel free to share with friends who will pray too.

#Prayforbert #godisgood #prayersmatter #winning
#itsthelittlethingsthatgetyou #hecaresaboutwhatyoucareabout

14

One Prayer Away from My Breakthrough

The prayer of a righteous man is powerful and effective.
James 5:16b

While attending a conference on how to pray for the sick, I bumped into an acquaintance. I knew she'd been struggling with a painful and debilitating condition. After exchanging pleasantries, I asked if she had gone forward to receive prayer for healing at the end of the last session.

"Oh no, I couldn't do that!" she responded.

When I pressed her as to why she was holding back, she blurted out, "I've been prayed for before with no relief. What if I don't get healed? What would that say about God's love for me?"

I wish this were a rare occurrence. It is not. Countless hurting people have given up because they did not experience the miracle they were hoping for. I know pastors who won't teach that God heals because they are afraid of disappointing their congregants. One of the most challenging things in healing ministry is the discouragement of those who don't receive their healing "suddenly." They often misinterpret their lack of a breakthrough as a rejection on God's part or some failure of their own. It is heartbreaking to watch someone in need turn down prayer because they've already received prayer.

It was this picture that God brought to my mind when He told me to never give up. He said, "Don't do this." Then he displayed that picture of my encounter with my friend's disappointment in my head.

He impressed upon me that every prayer does something, whether we see it manifest physically or not. Far too many people have given up one foot short of striking gold. Can you imagine a miner hitting the ground once or twice with his pickax and then declaring, "There must be no gold for me." That would be ridiculous. We would expect him to deliver hundreds of strikes, digging deeper and deeper until, finally, he could exclaim, "Eureka!" How much more priceless and valuable is supernatural healing. To think that each prayer isn't bringing us one step closer to our treasure is ridiculous. Unlike the miner, we aren't blindly searching. We already have the map and a guide, all we need is the faith to persevere.

This dynamic, of course, applies to every promise from God. Some treasure is easy, lying right where we can stumble over it but some, the most precious, is only attainable through the application of the persistence that faith supplies. Every prayer is releasing something in the supernatural. Every prayer is effectively bringing you closer to your breakthrough. Don't give up.

Prayer Illustration

Lord, What, if anything, have I given up on? Where have I walked away just short of breakthrough? I repent of any disappointment or anger I felt about the situation, and I ask you to help me begin praying again. Please help me to develop the perseverance I need to see a breakthrough. In Jesus' name, Amen.

Excerpts from my Facebook timeline:

03/23/2017

Daily Prayer reminder

Bert's scan is today to measure how effective his treatment has been. That's the official reason. We are excited to see how effective our prayers have been.

The book of James says the prayers of the righteous are powerful and effective. Since every believer is made righteous at the cross, we know there have been some powerful prayers said on his behalf!

Thank you for remembering to pray ! Please press like when you have prayed and feel free to share with friends of faith.

#Prayforbert #godisgood #prayersmatter #winning #movingmountains #goodreportonitsway #powerfulandeffective

04/15/2017

Daily prayer reminder

Today is that limbo day of holy week. The day after the crucifixion and before the resurrection. I can't imagine the despair and loss of hope the disciples experienced. Not understanding his forewarning, they had nothing to make them hopeful. It appeared God had abandoned them. The next day, everything changed forever. What a difference a day makes.

I am so grateful to be born this side of the resurrection! No matter how bad things seem, we never have to face a day like that Saturday so long ago. Believe me, it is this truth that carries me some days. The knowledge that he is always there, always good, and always victorious no matter what things look like.

Thank you for your prayers! Please press like when you have prayed and feel free to share with praying friends.

#prayforBert #godisgood #prayersmatter #winning #sadsaturday #cantbelieveeverythingyousee #heisalwaysgood #sundayiscoming

15
It's the Family Business

'My son,' the father said, 'you are always with me,
and everything I have is yours. Luke 15:31

When I first received salvation, we attended a mainline evangelical church. One of the popular things to do at the time was to take a spiritual gift "inventory" to determine where you were best suited to participate in the life of the ministry. I remember that almost everyone I knew that took that test scored very high in "service" or "helps." This result, of course, was simply a reflection of what gift they had operated most in, not a true expression of their predominant call. Washing dishes and weeding requires minimal risk and extend a low threshold for success. Most people can weed without God's help. Hence, many people gravitate toward "service" over other areas that require a greater dependence on the Holy Spirit.

Unfortunately, this kind of thinking only serves to underscore a sort of slave mentality in the Body of Christ. If we work hard enough to be pleasing, he may withhold his wrath and punishment. It's this mentality that often blames God for our circumstances and causes faith to fail in a crisis.

Much like the "good" older son in the parable of the prodigal son, we view ourselves as slaves in our Father's kingdom. "But he answered his father, 'Look! All these years I've been slaving for you and never disobeyed your orders. Yet you never gave me even a young goat so I could celebrate with my friends." Luke 15:29

When we see God as a demanding taskmaster, it's easy to blame him for our struggles. It's easy to believe he would "teach us" a lesson through a sickness like the early slave owners "taught" their slaves by whipping them. Easy, but not accurate. God isn't our slave owner; he is our father.

It is from this perspective that we understand that the Father, who has given us access to everything in the kingdom is not an abusive father who would curse us with suffering. It is in the context of the family we understand that more than anyone else, HE is for us, and we can't help but want to be pleasing in response. Not to earn his love but in response to being loved by him.

Whatever you are going through today, please be assured He wants only the best for you. Being a Christian has never been an inoculation against calamity. It is the promise of an ongoing relationship as you navigate troubled waters.

Prayer Illustration

Father God, make me aware of the times in my life I thought you were holding out on me, the times I thought you were punishing me to teach me, and the times I felt like a slave, not a son. What is your truth about those situations, Lord? Help me change the way I think and embrace the fullness of your love. In Jesus' name, Amen.

Excerpts from my Facebook timeline:

01/04/2017

Daily Prayer reminder

Today we are at the hospital for Bert's endoscopic biopsy of the mass in his pancreas. Expecting a good report.

Thank you for your love, support, and especially your prayers. Each prayer moves us closer to our breakthrough.

Please press the like button when you have prayed. Feel free to share with your friends to pray.

#Prayforbert #godisgood #prayersmatter #winning #goodreport #hemakesallthingsnew

Sitting here thinking as I wait for Bert. The last couple of days, a couple of things have stood out to me. The terms "God uses you" and "serving God" and I realized that I don't see myself in these terms. I don't expect to be used by God and I don't really serve him. Not like a servant would. I guess I just see myself as his daughter so much that these terms don't fit anymore. I have been invited into the family business. I'm not used so much as I am invited to participate. I don't really serve him, I just do what is natural to do as a daughter.

Every morning I make my mom coffee, ice water, lay out her medication and her newspaper. I am not serving her and she is not using me, it's just what you do when you love someone.

Just sayin' this is where I'm at.

06/06/18

Daily Prayer reminder

Jesus said we must become like children to enter his kingdom. I honestly believe that he would not require us to do something he's not ready to empower us to do. Many people believe that means we must become sinless. Although holiness is important, I don't think that's what Jesus meant. Let's face it, every toddler caught with a marker will deny their masterpiece when caught. For me, to be child like is to be innocently trusting. To not worry or strive but to trust my father to provide and protect. So many of us come to him later in life, damaged and guarded - self protecting. We receive forgiveness but continue to live from a position of wariness. He wants to restore our innocent ability to trust him. He is trustworthy. If you have served him but find it hard to trust him, I pray you invite him to restore what's been stolen - that innocent heart that can believe in miracles and angels and an unending, overwhelming ocean of love for you.

THANK you for believing for Bert's restoration. Bert and I believe your prayers are filled with miracles and healing. Please press like when you have prayed and feel free to share with praying friends or copy and paste. #prayforBert #godisgood #prayersmatter #winning #notme #ididntdrawonthatwall #childlikefaith #seedsofmiracles #weplantandhegrows #heistrustworthy

16

Lift up Your Eyes
(Seeing from God's Perspective)

For nothing is impossible with God." Luke 1:37

One of the characteristics of our western culture is how we draw conclusions based on facts. Especially when you're immersed in a medical or scientific environment. This characteristic isn't necessarily a bad thing but it can be limiting in the kingdom culture. Facts don't always take the invisible kingdom into account. This concept is a little weird considering how much of science is based on what was once unseen and invisible.

I once heard John Wimber tell of a study in which the following statements and questions were presented to two groups of people, one of which consisted of North Americans and one of which consisted of Asians.

Statements:

1. Cotton does not grow in cold climates.

2. England has a cold climate.

Question: Does cotton grow in England?

The North American group concluded that cotton did not grow in England because of the climate there. However, the other group responded that they could not know whether cotton grew in England because they had never been to England. In other words, facts do not always dictate what's possible.

In the same way, we as a people of faith understand that facts are only one level of truth and that as children of God, we live from a higher reality. For instance, science says when you die, you are done. Unlike in the movie "The Princess Bride," there is no such thing as mostly dead. Dead is dead. Unless Jesus steps into the room and says, "wake up" as in the case of Jairus' daughter, not to mention numerous accounts of the dead being raised by revivalists throughout the world in our day. Just one, for instance, is the account of Pastor Rego of Mozambique praying for the deceased wife of a co-worker in the book "Always Enough: God's Miraculous Provision among the Poorest Children on Earth" by Rolland and Heidi Baker. In the story, Pastor Rego shares how he was moved to pray for a miracle and how this wife and mother was brought back to life.

Even as you read this, there will be a temptation to look for a "logical" explanation of how something like this could be possible. I have an answer for you: God's perspective. In our culture, we say, "show me, and I'll believe." With God's perspective, we believe first, then we see. Through faith, we access possibilities that logic can't apprehend because it is limited to the known.

Ask God where you need his perspective in your life. Is it provision? Protection? Healing? Invite him to reveal his promise for that area of concern. What is heaven's solution for you? One of the ways I've learned to access God's perspective is to study how the miraculous trumps the natural in scripture. Another is to search out miracle stories on the Internet. A third way is to consistently testify to yourself. Make a list of the miracles you've participated in or the testimonies of friends that you know personally. This last exercise can be especially powerful simply because you "know" the people involved. Whatever the need, there is a testimony and an answer.

Prayer Illustration

Lord, I come to you with my concerns today and ask that you would remind me of my testimonies of your goodness in these areas. I ask that you would give me eyes to see your goodness today and send witnesses to me to encourage my faith. In Jesus' name, Amen.

Excerpts from my Facebook timeline:

01/09/2017

Daily Prayer reminder

Thank you for your prayers. God has been inundating me with this message.

LIFT UP YOUR EYES!

That was his word for me for 2017 - perspective. He told me to see things from his perspective. Then I'm reading a post from Joel Osteen and the message? Lift up your eyes. Bill Johnson preaches and a large part of what he preaches is about seeing what God is doing. Listening to a message from Mahesh Chavda on spiritual warfare - lift up your eyes. Last night, Tommy Tenney's message ended with lift up your eyes!

I think God wants me to lift up my eyes.

Psalm 121 pretty much says it all. Thanks Jan Parker for covering us with that!

Thank you for hanging in there with us. Thanks for helping us to keep our eyes above the problem and on the victory. Bert and I are so thankful for you! How easy it would be to focus on the immensity of the problem if not for your prayers!

Please press like when you have prayed and feel free to share with friends that will pray.

#Prayforbert #godisgood #winning #prayersmatter #lookingup

03/24/2017

Daily Prayer reminder

Being assailed by the devil this morning. Grrrrr. I know that miracles are not born out of fear. Miracles are born out of faith and Faith and fear cannot coexist so I am rejecting every thought of failure as soon as I recognize it. The key is to recognize those insidious thoughts that seek to weave themselves into the fabric of my mind and take them captive. Today I choose to focus on God's promise of life and life abundant.

I have been seeing doubles everywhere lately. I don't just find one quarter, I find one and then immediately find another. Double numbers on every clock face. I see it as God's promise of double blessing and it's right around the corner.

Bert has been experiencing discomfort in his stomach area when he eats or drinks. Please pray it goes away as it removes his motivation to eat and drink. I will be at retreat this weekend so I won't be here to nag him into eating, etc.

Thank you for praying for us. Please press like when you have prayed and feel free to share with your friends who will pray.

#Prayforbert #godisgood #prayersmatter #winning #doubleportionpromise #faithtrumpsfear #idlikemylifebackplease #tummyachesucks

12/31/2017

Daily Prayer reminder

Happy New Year's eve. As I pray into the new year I continue to hear "there is more" and "more is coming". There is so much potential in this promise - both for good or ill. It really depends on the perspective you live by. If I were to dwell on the loss and painful challenges of the past year, "more is coming" could create an atmosphere of fear and dread in my heart. However, because I choose to embrace the countless ways the lord has blessed us, "more is coming" creates excitement and anticipation of goodness for the coming year. I believe we will each experience more of his abundant goodness this year.

This morning as I was praying for each of the people who prayed for Bert yesterday, God reminded me that each prayer prayed is dismantling a stronghold the devil has sought to establish in our lives. Every single prayer uttered on Bert's behalf has increased his strength and extended his life. I could see the devil laboring to complete a block wall trying to lay blocks as fast as possible and every time a prayer was whispered, several would fall. There weren't many blocks left and the prayers of our friends were dismantling the wall faster than the devil could build. Thank you for each precious prayer!

Please press like when you have prayed and feel free to share with praying friends or copy and paste.

#prayforBert #godisgood #prayersmatter #winning #tearingdownwalls #releasinghealing #thereismore #moreiscoming2018

17
Delayed Answers

"Instead of their shame my people will receive a double portion,
and instead of disgrace they will rejoice in their inheritance;
and so they will inherit a double portion in their land, and
everlasting joy will be theirs." Isaiah 61:7

We live in the age of the immediate, and things are getting faster all the time. I can't count how many times I've chafed while waiting at the fast-food window or found myself tapping my toes in front of my microwave. When sixty seconds seem like an eternity, it's easy for discouragement to wrap itself around our minds like cling wrap suffocating our hope as we wait on the Lord to move on our behalf.

In the hallway of "waiting," I have to remind myself that my restitution is accruing interest. The Bible is full of instances where waiting meant an increased return. Consider the accounts of Sarah, Hannah, and Elizabeth in the Bible. Sarah, the wife of Abraham, didn't just become Isaac's mother, she became the mother of a nation. Hannah wasn't just Samuel's mom; she was the mother of a prophet, priest, and king maker. And Elizabeth became the mother of the greatest prophet of the Old Covenant and the forerunner of Jesus.

Yet, for each of these women, there was a period of "not yet." A barren, fruitless time. How easy, how very normal to despair of seeing their prayers answered. Of believing they had been overlooked and forgotten by God. But the answer was coming, and when it happened, it was extraordinary! In each of these scenarios, we witness the birth of a history maker. The conception seemed impossible, but the baby was exceptional.

What about King David? His beginning with God looked terrific. As a young boy, he's called in from the fields to be anointed king by the great prophet Samuel, chosen over his older brothers. Next, he accomplishes the impossible - the defeat of Goliath. Then he experiences mighty victories as a warrior for Saul, loved by the multitudes. Everything was made for love, as Bert would say. And then. Then comes the jealousy, the madness, and the persecution of Saul. Years of running, hiding, and rejection. In 1 Samuel 30, we find David at his lowest, rejected by his king, by his people, by the Philistines he had adopted and finally by the lawless men he's been leading. At this point in his life, it would have been justifiable to accuse God. Where was the crown? Where was the honor? Where was the promise? However, David does not give up hope. Instead of turning away, he pressed into God for strength and direction. That critical moment was a turning point of restoration for him. Once the promise came, it was for more than a kingship. In 2 Samuel 7, David is promised an eternal reign, eventually becoming the "father" of the promised messiah - God's son. David's promise of a kingdom had gained interest.

I remind myself of these things when I begin to feel forgotten or defeated. Like a snowball rolling downhill, God's delayed promises are gaining momentum and magnitude.

God wants to breathe life into the dreams you've shelved. One of the best things about the kingdom is that it is never too late, and nothing is hopeless with God. My first step to getting back on track is always confession and repentance. I confess my lack of hope in an area and ask him to change the way I'm thinking about it. In essence, I ask him to refresh my dream. I will make declarations about it, sometimes saying as Mary did, "I don't know how it will happen, but I believe."

Prayer Illustration

Lord, Please remind me of the dreams I've stopped dreaming and the prayers I've quit praying. Reveal every area where I've given in to despair and restore my hope. Help me to trust you to be faithful to the desires you've given me. In Jesus' name, Amen.

Excerpts from my Facebook timeline:
01/11/2017
Daily Prayer reminder
Running behind this morning because we had to get ready to come to the hospital for Bert to receive a portable catheter in his chest to facilitate chemo treatment. As we were leaving Dinuba, the clouds overhead released a deluge of rain. It was amazing! After years of drought, California's central valley water reserve is being restored with abundance. We have seen bridges and roads sink because of the drain on the underground water reserves, orchards abandoned for lack of water, water restrictions enacted, etc. But many of us pressed in through prayer and this morning my rain gutters were overflowing! God is reminding me that when answer to prayer is delayed, often it is because God is increasing the fullness of the answer. We are not overcome by the delay to Bert's healing because the fullness of His answer will be more than we can think or imagine! Thank you for your faithfulness and perseverance! We love you!
#Prayforbert #prayersmatter #winning #godisgood #letitrain

03/05/2017

Daily prayer reminder

Bert has had a couple of rough days. Can't figure out if he's dehydrated or his red blood cells are low. Going to check it out tomorrow.

So we have this amazing young woman in our church that has been looking to change jobs. She has been looking for a while with no doors opening. Long enough to justify some discouragement on her part but she has persistently said "I know God has something good in store for me." Sure enough, she landed her dream job this week with another offer on the table. God reminded me when I heard of her new job, that an answer delayed is gaining interest. That's what I'm claiming for us! Every day that goes by without complete healing means it's going to be even more amazing when it happens! Please press like when you have prayed and feel free to share with praying friends.

#Prayforbert #godisgood #prayersmatter #winning #thefutureisbright #accruinginterest #moreamazing #tiredbutstillkickin'

18
Who Is Setting Your Agenda?

Finally, brothers and sisters, whatever is true, whatever is noble, whatever is right, whatever is pure, whatever is lovely, whatever is admirable— if anything is excellent or praiseworthy— think about such things. Philippians 4:8

As a leader, in both secular and non-secular positions, I've had to attend a multitude of meetings. Some meetings are like holding my breath underwater, as some folks tend to love talking a thing to death. Patience is not my strongest trait. I'm kind of a "what's the bottom line - let's make a decision and do something" kind of girl. Sometimes this works well, and sometimes it backfires, but I will never be accused of timidity.

One of the first questions asked at any meeting is, "What's on the agenda?" It's another way of asking, "What will we focus on?" or "What will we be investing our time in?" An agenda establishes what issues the participants will concentrate on. The person setting the agenda is usually the one leading the meeting - the head honcho. The worst meetings are the ones where someone comes in with an agenda of their own. They will get everyone off track, and the meeting is not just unproductive, it is counter-productive.

I've found one of the hardest things for me is to take time to ask the Lord what his agenda is for the day. I mean, I usually start each day with a long list of things demanding my attention, and I like to "get' r done." I will be so focused on tackling the day before me that even when I spend time with God, I don't ask for the agenda. On these days, my God time has just become part of my schedule. Quiet time - check. This complacency is precisely the opportunity the devil is looking for to insert his agenda into my day. It may start with the driver in front of me going 15 miles under the speed limit and progress into unscheduled phone calls and broken appliances. Before I know it, my list is long, and my mood is dark. If I have the presence of mind to look for God's opportunities in the upsets of the day, the devil backs off, and my day just gets back on track.

One of the most consistent ways that I've seen the devil insert his agenda into someone's life is through illness. Every person who has experienced illness in any form can testify that your thoughts tend to be consumed with how crummy you feel. There is rarely an expectation of feeling better because we are in the "now" moment of misery. If you are dealing with a severe condition, focusing on your wretchedness is the first step in allowing the devil to cast his agenda for your future. If you feel this bad now, how much more so in the days to come? The more you zero in on your pain and discomfort, the more significant the increase. This effect is quite understandable. Pain hurts.

This concept applies to more than just physical pain. I remember one day after an unusually hard night; I was so tired. I just couldn't work up any energy. As I said to myself for the hundredth time that day "I'm exhausted," I had this thought, "Why are you exhausted?" Bear in mind a lack of sleep, being a 24/7 caregiver for my invalid mom, taking care of the needs of my teenager, leading a church and keeping up with Bert's situation might have been the answer. Instead I heard, "You're depressed. That's why you're tired." I was surprised at the thought because I don't tend toward depression. But the idea came again, and I said out loud, "I think

I'm depressed."

No sooner did the words come out of my mouth than I was enveloped by a thick, black kind of blanket in which I could barely breathe. The weight of those words wrapped around my body making it hard to move from my chair. I spent the day dragging myself from room to room just trying to do the bare minimum necessary to keep going. The harder I tried, the more tired I became, the more I embraced the thought of depression. Tears flowed as I considered the bleakness of our future. When I lay down that night, I said to the Lord, "Lord, I'm depressed." "No you're not. You're tired. Go to sleep." I did not have the energy to argue. I went to sleep.

When I woke up, the first thought I had was, "God says I'm not depressed." Getting out of bed, I didn't feel too bad. As I was brushing my teeth, I said, "God shaysh I'm not depreshed." I felt a little better. As I snuggled in my recliner to start my day with God, I said, "I'm not depressed." I experienced a lightness in the room, so I chuckled as I said, "I'm a happy person who has a lot on her plate." My connection with God strengthened, and I wasn't just saying I was happy, I felt happy. The atmosphere shifted because the agenda changed.

The devil plays dirty. He will use anything and everything to veer us off track. Whether it is sickness, pain, weariness, or offense, he is always looking for an opportunity to push his agenda. You know, the one that Jesus talked about - to kill, steal and destroy. If you find that you are spending your thoughts on how bad things are, take them to the Lord. I know this seems like an oversimplification but it's the only way to get back on track. If you're having a hard time connecting with his voice, try using your imagination. After all, God created your imagination. Think "what if" thoughts but with the best possible scenarios. Don't stop yourself with "those things are impossible" or "that won't happen." You are just imagining, so imagine the impossible with God. The devil has been using your imagination to paint the worst scenarios, so why not turn it around and just imagine the most beautiful, impossible, fantastic things you can. Go crazy. Then speak the truth; all things are possible with God.

Prayer Illustration

Heavenly Father, I want you to set the priorities for my day. Please help me to have the self-control to check with you before I establish my agenda. Give me eyes to see the ploys of the devil and to resist him at every turn. Let my first thought be to seek you whenever I face surprises or disappointments throughout today. Teach me to imagine with you as you lay out your plan for today. In Jesus' name, Amen.

Excerpts from my Facebook timeline:
01/28/17
Daily Prayer reminder
Thanks for your prayers and well wishes yesterday. Bert is more "normal" today than he has been the last 2 days. Up and around and actually talking! We were totally blessed yesterday - a young couple from our church sent us an amazing bouquet for our anniversary that really brought an air of joy into the room and then we went to dinner with 2 of our dearest friends. Bert didn't think he could make it to dinner but I pushed him and he was

so glad he did. Actually felt better than just dozing in a chair.

It would be so easy to retreat from living and just focus on cancer. Isn't that the devil's strategy? To get our focus off of the goodness of God and on to how crummy we feel? The good news is we have so many people praying for us that we overcome that strategy!

Thank you for helping us to be overcomers!

Please press like when you have prayed and feel free to share with your friends who pray.

#Prayforbert #godisgood #prayersmatter #winning #ihatethedevil #overcomers #iloveflowers

04/01/17

Daily prayer reminder

I think my sub - conscious must be leaking into my sleep. I keep dreaming I am in a war. It's a very nasty war where we are dodging bombs and tanks and flying shooting machines. Kind of like a mix of the terminator war and some alien sci-fi flick where we are the underdog. The good news is that the good guys always win in those movies and I am confident that we are winning too. However, I must confess I am tired. Working all day and fighting all night is wearing this soldier out! I find my temper is short and my compassion is low. Pray for my poor family!

Please pray for the joy of the Lord to increase in me today.

Bert on the other hand seems to be in good spirits today. And Audrey too. Even my mom (who is in a lot of pain from her back) is happier then me. Hmmmm. I think I need another retreat.

Thanks for your prayers. All of them. Please press like when you have prayed and feel free to share with praying friends.

#prayforBert #godisgood #prayersmatter #winning #grouchyisnotaspiritualgift #donthurttheonesyouliveeveniftheyirritateyou #thoushaltnotkill

04/18/17

Daily prayer reminder

The Lord spoke to me this morning about envisioning our victory. About using the eyes of my mind to prophesy healing. As I think about it, isn't that what the devil does? He crafts the worst case scenarios and plays them over and over in your head. The images we dwell on tend to direct our path. Today I choose to imagine with God. To visualize victory in every area of our lives. Instead of playing what if with the devil, I will play what if with the holy spirit. Like what if the testimony of Bert Boyd's healing becomes so well known he has to travel all over the world to speak? What if our healing anointing becomes so powerful, people line up around the block for prayer? What if he feels so good he never retires? What if he gains so much weight we have to find time to join a gym in between healing people and speaking to multitudes and selling millions of cases of grapes?

I invite you to join me in imagining with God as you pray for us today. Please press like when you have prayed and feel free to share with praying friends.

#prayforBert #godisgood #prayersmatter #winning

#daydreamingwithholyspirit #goodproblemstohave #iseevictory

#itsrightaroundthecorner #hesgoingtohavetoworkout #hahahaha

19

Self Protection Is Self Isolation

But the LORD God called to the man, "Where are you?"
Genesis 3:9

Everyone avoids pain. Everyone. I've heard it said that people are experts at avoiding pain. Even the poor, confused souls who embrace pain are using the pain they choose to avoid some other discomfort. For example, most cutters are trying to relieve the pain of stress or anxiety by focusing on the pain caused by cutting themselves.

Working in the ministry of inner healing, I've found one of the most common ways to avoid pain is to erect walls. We will put up a barrier between our consciousness and the painful events of our childhood. Sometimes our brain will recognize the potential for pain and redirect our thoughts away from the very things that need to be dealt with. They need to be dealt with because they are still there, festering. I picture it in my mind like a blob of radioactive material on the other side of a wooden fence, hidden but still pulsating death through the boards.

When I was a little girl, I was abused by the father of my best friend. I don't think it's necessary to go into all the details, but I learned from a very early age how to effectively wall off my pain. For years as an adult, I would hear the heartbreaking story of some woman's abuse and be completely unmoved. I can remember thinking, "Get over it. I did." Years later, in an inner healing setting, my wall came down, and I dealt with the damage of that event. Surprisingly, it wasn't the abuse that had hurt the most; it was the unacknowledged perception that my friend had betrayed my trust. A scenario that had been repeated consistently in my friendships and accounted for my distrust of other women. When the wall came down, God was able to speak to the pain, and it dissipated. The key was to choose to bring the wall down because God would not violate my self-protection.

I think this is why we believe sin cuts us off from God as if it had some power to keep God out. I've been taught that sin is so abhorrent to God that he will not allow us to come near him until we repent. It is like a chasm between God and us. I believe this teaching is in error. If you've read the Bible, you will find multiple stories of God interacting with people who were less than perfect. Abraham would be a prime example. Talk about self-protecting! He traded his wife to foreign kings on multiple occasions to ensure his safety. I call this a pretty big sin, but God called Abraham his friend.

I believe that we choose to stay separate from God because of our sin. Like Adam and Eve in the garden, we tend to hide from God because we are afraid to hear what he may think of our choices. Quite often, this a subconscious choice and easily rectified. Anytime I feel as if I'm having a hard time connecting to him, I ask him to reveal what's come between us. Without fail, he is kind to show me some incident where I've taken offense, been unforgiving, or acted entitled. The connection is restored with the repentance I've been subconsciously avoiding.

You must be wondering how I can correlate the separation that sin causes, with experiencing pain. I don't. To sin is a choice. Pain is not typically something I've purposely brought on myself or chosen. It is something that's been done to me. However, what I do with that pain determines how well I connect with God. If I've chosen to bury the pain, I will not want God to come along and expose it. So I wall part of myself off from him, and our connection suffers. If I choose to numb myself to my pain, I am also numb to his presence, which is love itself. In my effort to protect myself, I am choosing to isolate myself from the only one who can help me. I find myself alone in the wilderness, prey to the predator who has caused the pain in the first place.

Prayer Illustration

Father God, I'm feeling disconnected from you. What has come between us? (Take time to listen, repent, forgive, or whatever he directs you to.) Thank you that you don't turn your back to me even when I've drawn away from you. Please restore my peace. In Jesus' name, Amen.

Excerpts from my Facebook timeline:
1/29/17
Daily prayer reminder
We are so blessed by the families in our church! We really are like a family with the same heart beat.
Today as I entered worship I was having a hard time connecting with the holy spirit. As I pressed in, I recognized that I had developed the smallest callous around my heart. So slight that I wasn't aware of it until I was in the house of God. Then it came to light because I was out of step with God. He revealed that I had subconsciously put a barrier around my heart because Bert was so sick this week and I didn't want to experience the depth of my anguish at seeing him suffer. So I set aside that feeling and shut down just enough to make it difficult to sense God's voice. Praise God for our church and their hearts to worship. Their praise carried me to the

throne room where God was able to speak to my hurts.

Thank you for your intercession on our behalf. You, too, help us hear the Father speak words of healing and hope. How does a pagan or atheist cope with cancer? I can't imagine.

#Prayforbert #godisgood #prayersmatter #winning #ihatethedevil #onthewingsofpraiseandprayer #throneroomencounter

2/2/18

Daily Prayer reminder

Through out this season my mind has been under constant assault. I am bombarded daily with thoughts of hopelessness and failure. These are not my thoughts but sent from a despicable liar to steal hope and undermine faith. Unfortunately, quite often, my response is to self protect. To avoid fear and hopelessness by shutting down emotion, erecting a wall around my mind. I say unfortunately because even though I silence the liar, I also silence the voice of the Spirit. Emotionless, I become hardened to the pain of those around me, without empathy. Self protection is self destruction. I recognize I've done this when God seems to become distant. The truth is I have become distant, I have built a wall around my heart that he will not violate. Once I realize what is happening, I repent of the sin of self protection and enter his presence. It is there, within him that the liar is truly silenced and the lie exposed.

This has happened so many times that I have probably written this post before. Sorry for the repeat but I am always surprised to find myself reverting back to this instinct of shutting down and I am always filled with wonder at the stripping away of self-preservation that has to happen to know peace. His promise to me has not changed - Bert will not die from cancer. Every prayer prayed brings us one prayer closer to being done. Please press like when you have prayed and feel free to share with praying friends or copy and paste.

#prayforBert #godisgood #prayersmatter #winning

#selfprotectionisselfdestruction #inhispresencethereisfullnessofjoy
#stilllearning #stillwinning

20
I'm Bigger than My Problems

Two are better than one, because they have a
good return for their labor:
If either of them falls down, one can help the other up.
But pity anyone who falls and has no one to help them up.
Also, if two lie down together, they will keep warm.
But how can one keep warm alone?
Though one may be overpowered, two can defend themselves.
A cord of three strands is not quickly broken.
Ecclesiastes 4:9-12

It's funny how we tend to allow other people's perceptions of us to determine our value. In this past year, I've released my position to new pastors as I've stretched to step out on my own. I began this process of transition a year before Bert died, not out of incapacitation or in anticipation of grief but believing God was calling us to something greater. When Bert died, some people misinterpreted my decision to mean I couldn't handle my position because of grief, even some who had been in on the initial decision. In response, I began to see myself as pitiable. I then quickly became offended that anyone could deny what I'd accomplished and pioneered, the culmination of which was to launch someone else into ministry. The perception that I'd given up and retreated (even though I knew that was a lie) became a shadow that colored every future scenario. I was a quitter. I was less than. I was a loser. In response, I fluctuated between self-pity and defensiveness. I would expound my accomplishments over and over again in my head. Can I say this is not a healthy place to live?

Thank God for, well, GOD! Every time I would come into

agreement with these thoughts, God sent someone to encourage me with the truth. Some dear friend who reminded me that I'm going from victory to victory - not loss to victory. That I'm not starting over, I'm building upon. More importantly, their actions supported what they were saying in tangible ways. For these people, I am eternally grateful. They have been streams in the desert.

The worst part of this process is when I hear pity in the voices of the people I encounter. I detest pity. Seriously. Pity implies that you are pitiable. Who in the world wants to be pitiable? Not only that, but it often leads to self-pity, which is toxic. I refuse to be defined by my loss. I mean, that would seriously limit anyone's potential.

Right after Bert's death, I was chatting with a friend from Bethel Church in Redding about the future. He told me, "God is opening new doors for you. You are not done. From the first time I saw you, I said to myself, 'This is a queen, and she's got blood on her sword.'" Thank you. If this event must define me, I prefer to be seen as the woman who made the devil pay a high price for what he stole. Not the woman who "lost" her husband and retreated. Can you imagine if we judged our children's potential according to their setbacks or what's been done to them? "Yes, that's Nancy, she tried to walk once but fell and scraped her knees. Poor, poor Nancy."

I'm not pretending I'm unaffected by Bert's passing. That would be so ridiculous. I will never be the same! But my future is not determined by my worst day. If anything, I've come through a refining fire - stronger, smarter, and more determined to carry God's kingdom forward.

In the two years of his diagnosis, Bert continued to work full time. Both years, he sold close to two million boxes of grapes. Far more than any other salesman in his office. He was so proud of that! He was an exceptional man with tremendous favor. Usually, he wasn't competitive, but every week he would check the numbers and proudly tell me how far ahead of everyone else his sales were. It was important to him, although he knew his bonus would be the same as everyone else's. It was important because he didn't want to be seen as the guy with cancer. He wanted to be known as the guy who sold two million cases of grapes. Like it or not, how we are perceived by those around us impacts how we see ourselves. I urge you to find your tribe - the people who will share your passions and values. Friends whose only agenda is your growth and well-being. Friends who won't condemn your shortcomings but will have the love and courage to confront them to help you grow. Who will call out your greatness and allow you to call out theirs. A family where you're pulling together, cheering each other forward, and building one another up.

Prayer Illustration

Heavenly Father, I choose to put self-pity, pride, and defensiveness away from me. I want to be an equipper and an encourager. To whom are you sending me for mutual strengthening and building up? How can I tangibly exhibit my support for them as we run our race together? Bring to my mind my testimonies of receiving this kind of support to defeat the lies the devil would use to disable me. In Jesus' name, Amen.

Excerpt from my Facebook timeline:

2/02/2017

Daily Prayer reminder

We are in Roseville today at the River west coast gathering. It's great to see Bert enjoy being around good friends. You know you're with friends when the conversation isn't all about cancer. I am reminded that we are still amazing and anointed and glorious people who just happen to be under attack. As one friend put it, "man it sucks that you're going through this. So what's going on at church?" In other words "I care but I know you're still alive." I love that!

Thank you for caring enough to pray. We are thankful for friends like you. Please press like when you have prayed and feel free to share with praying friends.

#Prayforbert #godisgood #prayersmatter #winning #lifeismorethancancer #stillawesome

21
It's His Will

Some men brought to him a paralytic, lying on a mat. When
Jesus saw their faith, he said to the paralytic,
"Take heart, son; your sins are forgiven."
At this, some of the teachers of the law said to themselves,
"This fellow is blaspheming!"
Knowing their thoughts, Jesus said, "Why do you entertain evil
thoughts in your hearts? Which is easier: to say, 'Your sins are
forgiven,' or to say, 'Get up and walk'? But so that you may know
that the Son of Man has authority on earth to forgive sins...."
Then he said to the paralytic, "Get up, take your mat and go
home."
And the man got up and went home.
When the crowd saw this, they were filled with awe; and they
praised God, who had given such authority to men.
Matthew 9:2-8

In Matthew 9, we find the story of the four friends and the
paralyzed man. When confronted with the faith of his friends, Jesus
says to the paralytic, "Your sins are forgiven." Realizing he has
offended the religious people present, he says, "Which is easier - to
forgive sins or to heal?" He then tells the man, "Get up and go
home." I share this because, in this story, Jesus ties the forgiveness
of sins and healing together. I don't mean that he only heals the
forgiven, but the story implies that both require a supernatural act
of God.

I think this is significant in the healing ministry. I don't believe
I've ever met a Christian that believes that God cannot or will not
forgive sin. We often proclaim that Jesus died for the sins of the

world. Not some of the sins, not most of the sins but all of the sins. Not only all sin but for all time - pre-cross and post-cross. On occasion, I've come across people who struggled with believing that God's forgiveness was for them, but that has always been a pre-conversion conversation. Thanks to John 3:16, we boldly proclaim that whoever believes will not perish, but they will receive everlasting life. This principle is so commonly accepted we see it flashed at ball games and on the bottoms of soda cups.

Yet there continue to be believers that do not equate that "all in" principle to healing. Somewhere along the way, they came to believe that while salvation is freely given, healing is intermittent, conditional upon a mountain of faith, a spasmodic occurrence. Some folks believe the God who forgives and the God who heals are two different guys. One is all-loving, all compassionate, all accepting - in short, a mustard seed of faith kind of guy. The other is perhaps temperamental, allows suffering (or even causes it), a distant being who is indifferent to our pain with an expectation of us practicing a perfect godlike kind of faith to receive healing. I'm sorry if this offends you, but I just don't believe we see that kind of God in the person of Jesus. This Jesus, who said, "If you've seen me, you've seen the Father."

When we share the gospel, we have every confidence that God will freely forgive anyone upon a proclamation of faith. We don't present the good news with the thought, "I hope God really wants to forgive them." No. We are almost cocky about what we are offering them - eternal life. All they have to do is confess, repent, and believe then WHAMMO! They're going to live forever. Yet, when we are asked to pray for healing, we are deluged with all kinds of doubt and fear as to whether God will show up. Wow. That is mind-blowing when we consider the Pharisees were not shocked by the healing but offended at the thought of forgiveness. We have certainly gotten confused as we've tried to explain our lack of results.

I think when Jesus tied healing and forgiveness together, he was saying it's all part of the same package. The same fellow that came to die for the world also came for the healing of the world, and when we pray for healing, we can have the same confidence that it is always his will to see healing manifest. I know your next question will be, "Why don't we always see it manifest?" Honestly, I don't know. I don't think the fault is His. Whether I didn't have faith for the healing, the recipient didn't want the healing, the sickness was bigger than a single prayer, and required persevering prayer, I don't know. But I do know, the God who died to forgive us is the God who suffered to heal us. All of us.

Does God want to heal all diseases? Yes, just as he wants to forgive all sins. You can take that to the bank.

Prayer Illustration

Lord, I need a soul tune-up. Are there any sins I've tried to hide from you because I believed it would be impossible for you to forgive. (Confess anything He's highlighted to you and receive his forgiveness.) Is there are any diseases or sicknesses, you cannot or will not heal. (Again, I feel confident of his answer. Write it down. Press it deep into your heart. Be prepared to pull it out again, every time you pray for someone to receive healing.) Thank you, Lord. In

Jesus' name, Amen.

Excerpt from my Facebook timeline:

8/6/2017

Daily prayer reminder

Praying for several people this morning who are fighting serious illness. Sometimes I confess I pray quickly over this list of names, releasing healing but this morning the lord impressed on me that even though I don't know all of them, they are precious to someone. That to someone they are beloved family - fathers, mothers, sisters, brothers, husbands, wives. And so I lingered over each name praying for miracles to be manifested.

I know that whether my prayer is short and quick or longer and more thoughtful, it is the choice to partner with God that is powerful. God didn't remind me of the all these things so I would feel guilty about the times I have prayed quickly. He reminded me so I would know that HE desires to see them healed. That HE knows their names and that I am invited to participate in seeing his will manifested in their healing.

Thank you for your prayers for Bert. Whether they are short and sweet or long and lingering, they are powerful because you are partnering with a powerful and loving God to see his will come on earth as it is in heaven.

Please press like when you have prayed and feel free to share with praying friends or copy and paste.

#prayforBert #godisgood #prayersmatter #winning
#itsalwayshiswilltoheal #kingdomcome #willbedone #partneringwithgod
#heknowsyourname

22
Dismantling Roadblocks

For if you forgive men when they sin against you,
your heavenly Father will also forgive you. Matthew 6:14

In some healing circles, there is the thought that cancer can be caused by unforgiveness or bitterness. I don't know that I would say holding onto unforgiveness causes cancer, but I think it can impede healing. With this in mind, I asked Bert if there was anyone he needed to forgive. He said no, he didn't think so. Now my husband was one of the most easy-going guys in the world. If there were someone who held no grudges, it would be him. But I am a stickler, so I asked him to ask God if there was anyone he needed to forgive. A few moments later, Bert became aware of a young man that we had encountered that he needed to forgive. We went through the steps of forgiveness together and continued to pray for healing. Although we never saw his healing manifest, I am confident that it wasn't hampered by any unforgiveness in his heart.

Whenever I think of cancer and unforgiveness, I am often reminded of a woman I met at the licensing school I attended who had stomach cancer. She was a pleasant woman who professed a deep love for God and believed she was called to ministry. Unfortunately, some people did not agree that she was meant to be a pastor and told her so. This event wounded her deeply. Whenever she recalled their words, she was transformed from a sweet and loving minister to an almost unrecognizable ball of fury seething with anger and bitterness. I asked her once if she would consider forgiving these people to which she replied, "I will never forgive them." Beneath her calm exterior, there raged a furious rancor devouring her heart in the same way the cancer was eating away her body. She passed away a few months later, the disease spreading and consuming her life. I am not saying that her bitterness caused her cancer, but I believe it contributed to the rapidity with which it spread. Cancer feeds on chaos, on a lack of peace, and where there is unforgiveness, there is no peace.

I want to remind you of the story of Jesus and the paralytic. Jesus speaks to the man on the mat and says, "Your sins are forgiven." Some people think he did that to reveal his nature as the Son of God. I don't. I believe that Jesus was simply addressing the unforgiveness in the room. He was dismantling the roadblock to the man's healing. In Jewish culture, sin and sickness were practically synonymous. In context, it would be quite reasonable for everyone in the room to believe that God's response to sin was to inflict illness, and the paralytic deserved his situation. Unfortunately, people continue to embrace these beliefs today. Not only would the cultural expectations of the day have created an atmosphere of judgment, but the paralytic may have done something so shameful, he was unable to forgive himself. Recognizing the presence of unforgiveness and knowing it would impede the man's healing, Jesus extended forgiveness to clear the way. He removed the barrier to the paralytic's healing.

I share these two instances to emphasize the power and importance of living a life of forgiveness. Not just for what we've done but for what's been done to us. To forgive or not and to be forgiven or not is a choice, not an emotion, although it can evoke some powerful emotions within us. Too often, we believe we must feel an emotional release before we can release someone who has wounded us. This concept is backward thinking. More often than not, we must choose to forgive before we experience any kind of emotional freedom or healing. Like Jesus, we must dismantle the blockade to our healing.

Please don't hear what I am not saying. I am NOT saying illness is always caused by unforgiveness. I am NOT saying you haven't been healed because you have unforgiveness. I AM saying the failure to extend forgiveness or receive forgiveness will hold you back from the breakthrough God has planned for you. How can you know if there is something you need to forgive? Ask God. If there are people in your life that you have failed to forgive, he will show you. If something comes up, choose to trust God with it and forgive.

The following are steps that I use to help me move through the act of forgiving:

Prayer Illustration

1. Lord, I repent of (insert sin here i.e., anger, hatred, bitterness, unforgiveness, etc.), and I ask you to forgive me.

2. I choose to forgive (insert name here) for (insert what they did).

3. It made me feel (enter everything you felt because of what was done to you).

4. It was wrong for that to happen to me. (It is important to acknowledge how wrong the situation was. If it's not wrong, there's nothing to forgive.)

5. Today, I am choosing to put judgment of this in your hands. I release my judgment of them to you, and I ask you to heal my heart and set me free from their ability to

hurt me further.

I will often practice the "exchange" at this point. I give God my pain or sin to him and ask what he has in return. I always get better than I give.

I pray this brings healing to you - physically, emotionally, and spiritually.

Excerpt from my Facebook timeline:

09/05/17

Prayers are appreciated for my son in law too please. Battling another auto immune disease. This is from my daughter.

Daily prayer reminder:

Today, we were very busy decluttering our new Sunday school space. As I was cleaning and throwing away crafts that haven't been used in over 20 years, the thought occurred to me that clutter is a lot like unforgiveness. It takes up space inside us that can be used for something so much better. We hang onto it because somewhere deep inside of us, I think we're thinking "I'm going to need this someday." That -- I'm going to need it to remind me to be strong, or put up walls, or remind myself why this person is toxic to me. When all the time, it's just broken crap taking up room. I realized I've been holding onto a lot of clutter in my mind, and it's time to say goodbye to it.

And in the same way, when I looked at the bleachy clean and organized closet and felt relief this morning, my spirit is also feeling at ease.

""Come to me, all you who are weary and burdened, and I will give you rest. Take my yoke upon you and learn from me, for I am gentle and humble in heart, and you will find rest for your souls. For my yoke is easy and my burden is light."" Matthew 11:28-30 NIV

23

The Only Way to Finish Is to Start
(Denial Is Deadly)

"Ask and it will be given to you; seek and you will find; knock
and the door will be opened to you.
For everyone who asks receives; he who seeks finds;
and to him who knocks, the door will be opened. Matthew 7:7-8

Some people live in denial and call it faith. I don't believe that
is biblical. The Bible teaches us that Jesus healed everyone who
came to him. The key to healing was seeking healing, not denying
sickness.

Faith is dynamic, not passive. It is seeking, asking, knocking.
Once we have sought, asked, knocked there may be a "wait on the
Lord" period, but again the idea is active. It is more like "wait and
anticipate" as if you were waiting in ambush. When we knock on a
door, we don't then walk back down the sidewalk and remain in our
car. We wait on the step in the anticipation that the door will be
opened to us. Neither do we stand at the door and, by faith, say,
"There's not a door in my way." You will never realize a solution
unless you recognize there's a problem.

Neither does faith dictate how God has to respond to us. I'm
reminded of the classic story of the man caught in the flood. The
day before the flood, local sheriffs came to his home to evacuate
him, to which he responded that he would not leave.

"I'm not worried, God will save me."

Just as predicted, the flood waters rose, and the man had to
retreat to the second story of his home. A rescue crew came in a
boat and tried to convince the man to abandon his home.

"I'm not worried, God will save me," came his response.

The flood waters continued to rise with no relief in sight. Finally, the man had to move to the roof of his home, where he sat in the downpour. An emergency helicopter spotted him and hovered above while they let down the ladder for him to be saved.

The man waved them off, shouting, "I'm not worried. God will save me."

Finally, the waters rose to the point that the man could not tread water any longer and drowned. Immediately he was transported to heaven where he confronted the Lord.

"What happened? I waited on you in faith! Why didn't you save me?" he demanded.

The Lord responded, "I sent the rescue crew, a boat, and a helicopter. What more did you want?"

Listen, needing help isn't a sin, and it isn't a reflection of our faith level. To deny a problem is to deny God the opportunity to bless us with a solution. To demand the answer come in the form we designate is foolishness.

Prayer Illustration

Holy Spirit, I know denial can be about more than my physical health. Please tell me if I am in denial about anything. Is there an area in my life where I'm making room for sin.? Is there someone I need to forgive? Is there be something I'm not doing like praying with someone or growing in my gifts? (Whatever he reveals, be prepared to acknowledge your need and ask him for a solution. If he doesn't respond right away, stay alert, and flexible! He is faithful.) In Jesus' name, Amen.

Excerpt from my Facebook timeline:

02/06/2017

Daily Prayer reminder

Today is Bert's second round of chemo. He is scheduled for 12 over 6 months. Praying for no side effects this week.

We were just discussing some things he can do to minimize the discomfort in his mouth. It made me realize that it is very hard for him to engage in "owning" his care. No one likes to be constantly reminded there is something wrong with them. I have known friends who have ongoing medical issues rebel against the meds that they have to take because they just want to be "normal". Instead of being thankful for their help, the medicine becomes the enemy. Bert is not there, he just expects his body to deal with things normally but right now it needs all the help it can get.

It's like being under attack and not asking for prayer. There's help out there but we resist admitting we need help. Crazy but true.

I am glad to ask! Please press like when you have prayed and feel free to share with praying friends!

#Prayforbert #godisgood #prayersmatter #winning #justask #medicineisourfriend #gethelpalready

24
Don't Be Impressed
(The Opposite of Denial)

David said to the Philistine, "You come against me with sword
and spear and javelin,
but I come against you in the name of the LORD Almighty,
the God of the armies of Israel, whom you have defied.
1 Samuel 17:45

If denial is deadly, intimidation is toxic. The word "cancer" can create such fear. Even though the medical community has made great strides in treatment, there is still no cure. I remember the day after our initial meeting with the doctor; I looked up pancreatic cancer on the internet.

Don't ever do that.

I was devastated by the prognoses I'd read. If I'd accepted the available medical reports, I would have to believe there was no hope. None. Not a glimmer. Then when we found out that he wasn't just fighting pancreatic cancer but two other cancers so rarely found in the pancreas and liver that our oncologist said only 1% of cancer patients had that combination of diseases and all three were rated as the most aggressive.

Isn't that just like the devil? To send a Goliath in to strike terror into the hearts of God's people? To paralyze them into defeat before a battle is fought? How fortunate for us to have been in the healing ministry for over 20 years. We had seen so many things healed that we were only temporarily overwhelmed. Then we shifted our focus. No longer would we consider the size of our enemy but the size of our God.

We very purposefully began looking for blessing and goodness in the process. If there was no good news, at least we had scores of people praying with us, which is good news in itself. If we had a setback, we would remind each other of past victories and prophetic promises. The more we focused on God's goodness, the less we were intimidated. Our focus determined our mindset and directly affected our measure of hope. Still, we found it had to be intentional – both actively watching for goodness and rejecting the temptation to dwell on our problem took effort. For us, faith was not complacency but action. Faith was deciding to steadfastly set our face toward the direction we wanted to go.

Where do you need a breakthrough? Is it finances? Health? Relationships? Invest some time in researching testimonies in the area you need the greatest advance. Write out any time you've ever seen God come through for you in that area or other areas. Borrow testimonies from your friends. The more space you give the reality of God's goodness, the less space you give the devil.

Prayer Illustration

Thank you for the times you have come through for me (speak out your testimonies). I believe if you've done it before, you will do it again. I praise you as the God of the breakthrough. In Jesus' name, Amen.

Excerpts from my Facebook timeline:
02/10/17
Daily Prayer reminder
I don't believe in living in denial but I am reminded that I cannot afford to be impressed by the size or severity of this problem. In other words, we

can't focus on how big or bad this disease may be. We must fix our eyes on God's goodness. Why? Because our focus determines our direction and we take on the characteristics of what we study. We don't just believe he is good, it's not a catchy slogan. We know he is good because we look for and see His goodness all around us. And when we can't see, we reflect on what we've seen before. You are a great part of helping us to see His goodness surround us. You are partnering with a good God and we love you for helping us to keep our eyes on Jesus.

Thank you for all your prayers. They are priceless.

Please press like when you have prayed and feel free to share with praying friends.

#Prayforbert #godisgood #prayersmatter #winning #fixyoureyesuponJesus

03/30/2017

Daily Prayer reminder

I have been reminded that it is a favorite strategy of the devil to steal your hope by magnifying the size of your problem. I'm sure that's what he was doing when we received Bert's final diagnosis as an extremely rare form of cancer. The temptation was to believe it was so bad that was hopeless. Which is ridiculous. God is not intimidated by rare cancer or any cancer. Our God is bigger than our problem.

Your prayers have helped us remember that truth in our more challenging moments. I am glad to report that Bert Boyd had a good day with minimal side effects from the Neulesta shot.

Thank you for strengthening us with your prayers. Please press like when you have prayed and feel free to share with your friends who will pray.

#Prayforbert #godisgood #prayersmatter #winning #thethiefisaliar #bigbiggod #strategyfail #moregooddayatocome #yourprayerscarryinghope

25
Not an Option

Then Jesus told his disciples a parable to show them that they
should always pray and not give up. Luke 18:1

One of my favorite movies is Galaxy Quest. It's based on the premise that a television show about space exploration is picked up by an alien planet who mistakenly believes that the show is an actual documentary. They come to earth seeking help from the crew against a brutal enemy. The tagline of the show was "never give up, never surrender." As the movie unfolds, it becomes clear the actors do not have the resolve or courage reflected in the roles they've played until the faith of their new friends inspires them to become like the characters they have portrayed. The movie uses humor to make you consider the cost of giving up. In the film, the price wasn't just surrendering their freedom to the bad guy; it wasn't merely the annihilation of a whole people group; it was also the loss of their innocence, hope, and faith.

Like the rings in a pond when you drop a rock in it, our choices create a ripple effect that touches countless people for generations to come. Like it or not, people are watching us - what we do, the choices we make. Even when we think no one is watching or affected, there is a spirit realm that reverberates from every decision we make, whether we see it or not. If we could apprehend the truth of this one thing, we would understand the significance of generational patterns of sin and blessing. Everything we do or don't do enriches or depletes our family legacy. Choices we make believing they only affect us are, in reality, influencing the spiritual future for those who follow us.

We decided early on to commit to life. We didn't do this lightly or thoughtlessly. We knew it would cost, but anything less would result in the unthinkable. We began saying to each other, "never give up, never surrender" as a way to encourage faith. The discipline of commitment costs, but the rewards are immeasurable. As I write this, I acknowledge we didn't experience the breakthrough we'd hoped for, but I know that our commitment to stand and not resign has inspired and encouraged scores of people. Even more so, it has been an investment in the spiritual inheritance of our family, faith family, and those to whom we have been spiritual parents.

We all have times in our lives where we quit short of the finish line. The good news is that our Father is the God of restoration. If any of those times have come to mind, ask God to forgive you. Ask him to brush off any shame or condemnation attached to the memory. Ask him what he wants to restore to you in place of the shame or guilt. Do this for each memory that surfaces. Declare over yourself, "From this day forward, quitting is not an option!"

Prayer Illustration

Lord, Please reveal any time that I have given up or given in. Please forgive me for not believing in myself or not believing in you enough to see the finish line. I ask you to wipe out any shame or condemnation that has attached itself to this event. Strengthen me to finish well from this day forward. In Jesus' name, Amen.

Excerpt from my Facebook timeline:

02/12/2017

Daily Prayer reminder

The thing about cancer that I've observed is that it wears you down. It isn't only physically draining, it is emotionally draining and an exhausting spiritual battle. The temptation to give up and find rest becomes greater the longer you are engaged.

Marriages that last are the ones where divorce is just not an option. No matter what is going on, there is a mindset that we will not walk out but we will work it out. As soon as divorce becomes an option it seems inevitable. That is why Bert and I declare that death is not an option. Life only. Period. We have seen the goodness of God and expect to see it increase in the land of the living. Psalm 27.

Thank you for standing with us and helping us to stand. Please pray for my friend Sonya. She has been fighting this fight for a year and she is tired.

Please press like when you have prayed and feel free to share with friends who pray.

#Prayforbert #godisgood #prayersmatter #winning #notanoption #inittowinit

26

The God of Fulfilled Promises

The one who calls you is faithful, and he will do it.

1 Thessalonians 5:24

When Bert was initially diagnosed, God told me he would not die. I suspect that is partly why Bert's death took me by surprise. What I mean is that I believed up until a few days before his passing, he would be healed of cancer. In spite of the evidence of his decline, I firmly clung to the hope of a miracle. I had this expectation mainly because I'd witnessed so many miracles since becoming a believer. When the miracle didn't happen, sub-consciously, my faith took a real hit.

I didn't realize the damage that had been done until I was at home alone, applying makeup and singing along with a song that had the phrase "you keep all your promises." I muttered to myself, "Well, all but one." My first thought was, "Did I just say that out loud?" My second thought was, "Do I honestly believe that?" After examining this speculation, I had to admit to myself that I did indeed believe God broke his promise to me. I decided not to pursue that particular train of thought right then, but it found its way into my consciousness time and again over the next few days until I could no longer suppress it effectively.

As I sat soaking during my quiet time, I asked him, "Father, why did you tell me Bert would not die?" He responded, "He didn't die." A picture of the day in question flashed in my mind. I could see me asking, "Is Bert going to die?" and I knew that at that moment, I had been asking, "Will he die right away?" I hadn't asked, "Will Bert be healed?" or "Will cancer kill Bert?" Then a slideshow of memories from our last two years together ran through my mind's eye, reminding me what a gift those years were.

"Bert didn't die - then," God said. I knew what he was saying. Everyone dies some time. His promise had not been that Bert would outlive me, it'd been for more time.

What a gift those two years were! In my grief support group, I am surrounded by many people who lost their spouses suddenly, with no warning, and it is tragic. They've left behind young children, debt, spouses who'd give anything to be able to express their love and appreciation one last time. Bert and I were able to travel, make memories, say everything you could want and more, and to secure a sizable life insurance policy to ensure I would not be straddled with debt in his absence. Bert had not died until we'd had time. As that slideshow played in my memory, I realized how faithful God had been to enable us to have time together - how Bert had not died.

You may think this is just semantics. Maybe it is. However, I am at peace with God. His promises don't always fit in our box. His miracles aren't always as we prescribe - how else could anyone have missed the Messiah. For me, he continues to be the God of miracles, and he continues to keep all of his promises.

Pray and ask God if there are any areas in your life where you harbor disappointment with him. Trust him enough to be honest with him. Invite him to speak into any circumstances that come to mind. Invite him to bring healing to any pain that has lingered because of your disappointment.

Prayer Illustration

Heavenly Father, Please bring to mind any disappointment I am holding against you. What do you have to say about that situation? (Take time to receive his truth regarding the circumstances you are struggling with.) Where were you or what were you doing when I needed you? Please heal my heart and restore my faith. In Jesus' name, Amen.

Excerpt from my Facebook timeline:

10/9/18

Daily prayer reminder

Sometimes, when I talk to people about Bert Boyd being healed I will see this funny look on their face that I'm sure they didn't mean for me to see. The look says, "I'm praying God gives you more time, no pain, strength and comfort. But a miracle? I'm afraid you're in denial." Once I see that look, I find myself becoming defensive. I want to convince them that God is still in the miracle business but I know they are only drawing from what they have experienced in their walk of faith. Either no one has taught them how to risk disappointment or their disappointment has taught them not to risk. Bert and I have been so fortunate to have experienced the miraculous! Once you do, the devil can no longer limit you. Then the scripture "anything is possible for him who believes" becomes truth. "With God, all things are possible" becomes more than just words. When Jesus said in John, "unless you see miracles, this generation will not believe", he wasn't condemning us for needing to see. He was making an observation of human nature. Most of us need to SEE before we dare to hope. Then we can say, "what he's done before, he will do again." I'm pressing in for this miracle because I love my husband but I'm also pressing in for the sake of my friends to SEE and experience the impossible made possible.

Thank you for agreeing with me and with God's word that anything is possible!

Please press like when you have prayed.

#prayforBert #prayersmatter #godisgood #winning #miracleshappen #doitagainlord #inaninstant

27

Why Are You Showing Me This?
(Releasing the Opposite Spirit)

Bless those who persecute you; bless and do not curse.

Romans 12:14

Prior to being appointed as a pastor, I was required to take Bible classes at a seminary. Nothing I'd been exposed to before that time had prepared me for the extreme liberalism that I would encounter there. I was shocked at the things being embraced and taught by the professors.

Upon my return home, I was asked by my Senior Pastor what I was learning. "I refuse to learn anything from them! They have nothing to teach me," I responded in tears, vowing I would not go back.

"No," he replied, "you're learning what we don't believe." He'd just given me a lesson on how to see in the opposite spirit. Unfortunately, it took years before I found someone who could articulate this lesson in a way that I could apprehend it.

I returned to that school with a different purpose - to not only learn what I did not believe but to be able to articulate back to my professors what I did believe and why. In retrospect, I don't think I changed their minds, although there were a few that did pause to consider what I was saying. Such as the professor who declared God was powerless. I asked, "If you believe God is powerless, why do you still pray?" (We'd just prayed for a classmate at the professor's request.)

He stopped for a moment. "I don't know," he said, looking puzzled. I doubt that he was swayed, but it did make him reassess what he was teaching.

This new perspective, this new way of seeing the negative and pressing into God for the opposite, was for more than my academic survival. After all, I wasn't the only student in those classes. I was, however, the single student in my classes who dared challenge (politely) what was being taught. God had placed me there to speak out the opposite of what was being established. Although I had little effect on my professors, I believe I helped many of my classmates retain their faith simply by reminding them there was a higher authority.

Sometimes when I encounter someone I've never met, I will sense something negative about them. I can meet a man and immediately know he's having an affair or hold hands with someone to pray and know they are struggling with rejection. It often turns out that what I've sensed is true. I used to think it was a keen sense of intuition. I believed it was a special gift given to me to avoid "bad" or broken people.

After my salvation, I hated knowing these things. I would believe it was a critical spirit rising up in me, highlighting the worst in people. I would pray over and over for the Lord to take this negative and critical spirit from me. This negative bent was especially distressing in light of the fact that Bert only ever saw the best in people. He would say something nice, and I would always have a "Yes, but I think they have issues with, etc." These occurrences would eventually be followed by shame and guilt over being so critical and a new prayer for deliverance. But being critical did not explain the accuracy of my perception. It wasn't until I heard Graham Cooke teach on the opposite spirit that I fully understood that it was God revealing these negative things and the reason behind it.

Just like my experience at school, I needed to see a higher purpose for this information. God isn't revealing the worst in people to cause me to turn away or avoid them. It's not meant to be some "secret knowledge" but to become the catalyst for me to press in for his truth. It is a revelation meant to spur greater intercession in private and bolder declarations of the opposite in public.

When we discern what the devil has done in a person's life, we have received our most effective weapon against his plans. First, by praying for them to be free of whatever is hindering them. Second, by initiating new possibilities through prophesying or declaring the opposite potential over them. It helps to remember that God has a plan for our life, and the devil has a counter plan. The counter plan is almost always the exact opposite of what God has planned for us. So when we see devastation in someone's life, it is usually the opposite of what God intended for them and gives us a key as to what God wants to happen in their life.

For the man having an affair? I would probably declare something like, "God created you with a great potential for faithfulness as a man who keeps his promises. I see he has given you the ability to carry kingdom authority because you are faithful and loyal to your word and his."

The woman struggling with rejection? "God is showing me he has poured out his favor upon you and is going before you to open doors you're not even aware of. He is opening your eyes to his favor upon you. Just like the aroma of freshly baked bread stirs mouth-watering anticipation of the meal, the aroma of favor upon you will fan into flame hunger for his kingdom. Watch and see how his favor rests upon you!"

Mind you, I only make the declaration God gives me to make, and it is always in the opposite spirit of what I've discerned the devil is doing.

Why have I included this particular piece in this book? You can't imagine the onslaught of harmful and destructive things the devil and barraged me with since Bert passed away. Opposite spirit declarations over myself have been one of my greatest weapons. Yes, I make them over myself too. After all, we are our own worst critics. If I'm willing to fight for others, I must believe I'm also worth fighting for.

Prayer Illustration

Lord, give me the discernment to push past the negative I see in the people around me and see them with your eyes. Please help me to call forth the great things you created them to do and be. Give me declarations that will open their eyes to your destiny and purpose and repudiate the lie of the devil in their life. In Jesus' name, Amen.

Excerpt from my Facebook timeline:

7/19/2018

Daily prayer reminder

You may find this hard to believe. Bert and were having a conversation and he was being kind of negative. That's right! The golden boy was being negative. Anyway I said something like "can't you be a little more positive?" to which he replied "I'm sorry. Some of us have to live in the real world." I just want to say, being negative does not mean you're more realistic. It means you're more negative. I think you can find hope in any situation. If I didn't see life filtered by hope I would have called it quits a long ago. I'm glad today was my day to be hopeful. It totally made me feel superior! Pray for my sweetie. He is totally grumpy. Please press like when you have prayed and feel free to share with praying friends or copy and paste.

#prayforBert #prayersmatter #godisgood #winning #grumpypants #hecouldbeadwarf #todayismysuperiorday #abouttime

28

The Cost

Suppose one of you wants to build a tower. Won't you first sit down and estimate the cost to see if you have enough money to complete it? Luke 14:28

There is a cost to obedience when you agree to surrender your will to someone else's will. Surrender isn't all that hard when you agree with the person to whom you've surrendered. But when you are not in agreement, giving up what you want or how you want something done can be quite challenging. I can't count the number of times I've wanted to take action, but God said to wait. Or how often I've had to step out in blind faith when I wanted to wait and see. Jesus warned his disciples that following him had a cost and urged them to consider it before committing to the road before him. The price can be as high as broken relationships and as insignificant as the discomfort of talking to a stranger.

There is also a cost to disobedience. Under the Old Covenant, disobedience was clearly defined by rules and, later, by Jewish traditions. The consequences of breaking the covenant could be quite harsh. Under the New Covenant, we're exhorted to live according to the law of the spirit where there is no black and white. There is only the whisper of the holy spirit drawing out the best in us but is also a whisper that is quickly and easily denied.

I recently spoke at a friend's church, where I shared testimonies of healing from some of my trips abroad. One of the most exciting was the restoration of sight to those who were blind or losing their vision. The first experience I had with that was in Brazil.

Upon arriving in Brazil, I had a dream where Jesus told me to kiss the eyelids of blind people, and their sight would be restored. I shrank at the thought of kissing eyelids. I was unfamiliar with the culture and knew people back home would be turned off by it. I decided that it wasn't actual kissing he wanted as much as praying for the Holy Spirit to come kiss their eyes. I would pray but no kissing on my part, thank you. As we gave words of knowledge, I shared my dream and invited the seeing impaired to come forward and receive healing. Many people came to me but no one's eyes were healed. Other things got healed but not eyes. That's how it continued throughout the week — lots of healing but not eyes. On the last night our team leader, Bill Dew, announced we could not minister healing in the customary manner of lining up at the front and inviting the sick forward for prayer because it was too crowded - standing room only. He decided we would do a fire tunnel for healing and trust God. However, one young man with his elderly mother in tow made his way through the crowd to Bill and petitioned for prayer for his mom, whom he'd brought a long way to receive healing. Bill relented and sent my interpreter and me out to the children's courtyard where there was room to pray for her. Asking what she needed prayer for, I was told she was blind in her right eye due to brain surgery, and he was desperate for her to be healed. This was it! My last chance to see the dream actualized. So I prayed my best prayer and asked if there was any difference. No. Then I heard Holy Spirit say, "kiss her eyelid." Determined to see sight restored, I explained via the interpreter what God was saying and asked permission to kiss her eyelid.

"Of course," she said.

I felt a little foolish at how hesitant I'd been in light of her enthusiasm. I prayed again and leaned forward and lightly kissed her closed eye. Opening up, she exclaimed she could see gray and vague shapes! We were so excited! I prayed again and planted a big old kiss on her eyelid. She opened her eyes and declared, "Yes I see clearly."

We tested it by covering her good eye and having her count the fingers we held up. The verdict was, yes, she could see clearly. Having received what they came for, mother and son left for home satisfied. My interpreter, Maria, and I went crazy in that little courtyard. We had gotten to participate in a miracle. Since then, I've successfully prayed for restored sight several times.

Because of that testimony in my friend's church, I was asked to pray for a little girl who was legally blind. She was timid and would not look at me or allow me to touch her. No eyelid kisses for her. So I sat down by her mommy and prayed a short, simple prayer. Her mom slipped off her thick lenses and asked her how many fingers. She responded correctly. Being a little further away, I held up my fingers, and again she answered correctly. She was smiling now; she liked this game. Mom sent her brother halfway down the aisle. How many fingers? Five. Yes! Thank you, Jesus. According to my friend, the family was only visiting, and there is no way to confirm her healing, but I'm claiming those five fingers as confirmation.

I was reflecting on this and how amazing God is during my quiet time the next day. I reflected on my experience in Brazil and how thankful I was for that miracle. Then God reminded me of the scores of people I had prayed for in Brazil but had been too embarrassed to kiss. I could see one young woman in particular who was losing her sight and had been desperate to be healed, and I knew God was showing me the people who had been cheated out of healing because of my disobedience. My vanity had robbed her of the healing my obedience would have released.

I heard, "There is always a cost to disobedience, and sometimes you are not the one who pays the price." I cried for a long time after that.

As I consider this, I can't help but think of Bert, who also did not get his healing. I would hate to think that Bert's healing didn't happen because of someone else's failure to risk, but I know it's a possibility. One thing I know - I can't unsee that desperate young woman who didn't get healed. Neither can I unhear the voice of the Lord, saying, "There is always a cost to disobedience." Please, God, help me to hear and obey.

Prayer Illustration

Holy Spirit, Please forgive me for the times I've intentionally ignored your voice out of fear. I don't want to be disobedient and rob others of a blessing. Help me to recognize what I'm afraid of and why. Give me a plan to overcome my fear and bless me with courage. In Jesus' name, Amen.

Excerpts from my Facebook timeline:
11/11/2018
Daily prayer reminder
The lord is speaking to me about simple faith this morning. Sometimes I'm too much in my head. What I mean is I often will hear something or learn something and think "yes that makes sense because it lines up with this." But then there are times I think "how does that work? It's inconsistent with

what I already know." It's good to test a teaching but sometimes I can demand too much proof. It is then that I must choose to trust his voice and just believe because of I witness the fruit of the thing. I encounter innumerable situations in the natural where I am trusting in technology I don't fully understand. I don't understand the law of lift but I trust it every time I get on a plane. I don't really understand electricity but I keep plugging things into the wall. Because they work when I do. God is not asking me to swallow every kooky thing out there. He is asking me to trust Him to keep me from error and just believe. To stop building cases for or against and trust his voice and rest in faith. He is taking me forward to a simpler perhaps superior form of childlike faith.

Bert Boyd says he hurts all over this morning. I think it may be old age. Thank you for your prayers! Please press like when you have prayed.

#prayforBert #prayersmatter #godisgood #winning #stilllearning #hisvoice #painpaingoaway

10/6/18

Daily prayer reminder

God had been impressing me with the significance of each person this morning. It's easy to think you don't matter but he has a destiny for you that was written the moment you were conceived. It's our decision to step into that destiny or to step away from it. Whether we pursue God's plan for us or allow the devil to lead us away from it, everything we do is significant one way or the other. We are not accidental events living encapsulated lives in isolation of insignificance. Even if we were able to live a clam like existence, our inactivity has an impact because we are not doing something that should have been done. Your prayer may be the prayer that moves the mountain. Your kindness, your encouragement, your smile may be the one that prevents the next school shooting. You are significant! Wrap your mind around this and step into your God given destiny today.

Your prayers for Bert Boyd are significant to us! They are defeating the principality of cancer! Thank you! Please press like when you have prayed. #prayforBert #prayersmatter #godisgood #winning #saturdaymorningmusing #youmatter

29

Honor - The Revelation of God's Love

My command is this: Love each other as I have loved you.
John 15:12

Even at (ahem) my age, I realize there is always more to learn. If I had to make a list of the most important lessons I've learned, I think honoring people would be right at the top.

I hate when people hand me a book and say, "You need to read this." Ugh. I have enough unread books to work through, thank you. So when I received Fawn Parish's book on honor, I was slightly irritated at the giver. By accepting it, I now felt I was obligated to read it. Thinking back on it, I'm embarrassed at my lack of appreciation. It proved to be one of those books that impacted me profoundly and established one of my lifetime core values. The title was "Honor - What Love Looks Like," and in it, Fawn avers there is a portion of the image of God in every person and honoring that is an expression of love. In other words, it's always possible to treat people with honor even when we don't experience warm fuzzies.

Following Bert's death, I've been so much more aware of how loving and healing are tied together. Probably because he submitted to receiving so much prayer ministry as we fought for healing. As painful as it was to have to be on the receiving side, it was also very enlightening. Far too many times, I watched him become a project - an accomplishment - to the person doing the healing.

While we are hungry for people to receive healing, I think we should remember the point is to make them feel loved as they are healed. I have known folks in their zealousness to see healing happen completely ignore the discomfort or embarrassment of the people receiving prayer. "What is your pain level now?" is a great way to measure the degree of healing that's happened. Unfortunately, it can also become a catalyst for performance by the recipient to escape the well-meaning but insensitive healer. I'm not suggesting we give up easily. However, I think it's essential to take the time to explain to people why we're persisting. It's also important to remind them God loves them and wants to see them healed. We must care as much about their emotional response as their physical response because the most important thing (to me) is that they encounter God's love as they are healed.

I don't think we have to sacrifice one for the other. Sometimes persistence begins to feel more like belligerence, and it fails to convey value for the person receiving prayer. When healing doesn't happen, it can make you believe something is wrong with you, you're not worthy, or God doesn't love you. These mindsets can effectively shut you down and keep you from receiving his healing, which means your persistence is hindering healing.

I also believe keeping love at the forefront keeps us humble. I try to ask myself, "Do I love this person?" before I minister healing. I do it to remind myself of WHY I'm ministering healing. To remind me of why Jesus healed. Love. He loved those he encountered. He felt compassion for them. He wanted them to experience wholeness and freedom from the degradation of disease. He didn't see them as another chance to exhibit his great anointing. They were not future testimony opportunities. They were people worth stopping for.

I confess, there have been times I've also continued to press in even though I could see the desire to escape in the eyes of my victim, er, I mean patient. I just knew if I prayed enough, they would be healed. Unfortunately, that look in their eyes would often change from wanting to escape to a firm determination to not get healed. The resentment of being held captive overruled their desire to be healed.

Seriously, it is so important to take the time to honor people as we pray because we haven't come so far in revival that everyone gets healed. I've only heard one person claim a 100% healing rate, but I've never witnessed it in my ministry. If I express love by honoring the person I'm praying for, the recipient is less likely to walk away feeling like a failure. Feeling loved inspires hope. Hope is the seedbed of faith. And faith will be more apt to believe, "I'm one prayer closer to my breakthrough."

Prayer Illustration

Heavenly Father, Please help me to see your image in the people I pray for. I want to honor you in them as I pray. I don't want to lose sight of their dignity and worth in my pursuit of healing. Give me a greater sensitivity to minister in love as you increase my anointing to heal. In Jesus' name, Amen.

Excerpts from my Facebook timeline:

4/17/18

Daily Prayer reminder

Bert and I were discussing how important honor is. One of the most wonderful things about my husband is how he honors everyone he encounters - from the least to the greatest, he always treats people with honor. He sees the person, not the position. I have heard many people talk about a culture of honor but Bert is one of the few people that I have seen actually create a culture of honor in whatever situation he is in. It has served him well, resulting in unexpected favor in many ways. Don't misunderstand, he doesn't have an agenda to garner favor. He simply has honor for people. When I was a young (and drop dead gorgeous) single mom working for a grape shipper, Bert would drop by my desk to chat. He didn't come by to hit on me like most of the buyers would. He just wanted to acknowledge the girls in the office before being shmoozed by the sales staff. He made you feel significant. I even told my co-worker, "If I ever get married again, it will be to a man like him." Never underestimate the power of your words. Or the power of honor. Although I had many suitors, Bert is the one that made it home to meet the kids.

Now after 32 years, I realize I still have so much to learn from this husband of mine. Lol. If you know me, I'm pretty sure you'll agree I have a lot to learn. Let's pray he lives long enough - say, another 32 years? Please press like when you have prayed and feel free to share with praying friends or copy and paste.

#prayforBert #godisgood #prayersmatter #winning #cultureofhonor #peoplematter #yourwordshavepower #stilllearning

8/13/2018

Daily prayer reminder

One of the things the devil will barrage me with are feelings of insignificance. He will tell me over and over that I don't make a difference. DON'T BOTHER TELLING ME THAT'S A LIE! I already know it's a lie and where it's coming from. Every once in a while, though, it feels true. Day before yesterday, I was at Walmart. I had a poor experience with the pricing on some items on the clearance aisle. They rang up full price. I told the cashier I would not take them and she should report them because they were on clearance but were ringing up full price. She responded, "I don't know they were on clearance." "No," I said, "I know you don't know that,

that's why I'm telling you. You should report it so it gets corrected." "But I don't know that they were." "I just told you, that's where they are and they are not ringing up as clearance. That should be reported so it gets corrected." "But I don't know that they are on clearance." This conversation was bad enough but throw in an attitude of judgement and shame because you are clearly trying to rip off her store and I just wanted to scream, "I am a good customer and worthy of honor you **?!*." This was just the cherry on top of a series of events that have disappointment, dishonor and frustration attached from the past week. Events that have pierced my heart, kept me awake at night and made my stomach hurt. In comes the devil with his litany - you are insignificant - you are powerless - there is no justice for you - there never will be.

I would like to say, I shook him off. Honestly, instead I went to the Lord and laid out all my feelings and he responded. "Will you praise me in the valley?" Seriously? I don't feel like praising. I feel like getting people fired. I feel like screaming and yelling and saying mean things and crying (which I have done) and shooting someone (not fatally) and cussing and plotting revenge and feeling sorry for myself. However, I did begin to praise. Not from emotion but from discipline. From intellect not heart. I praised him in direct contradiction of what I felt. Then I got a phone call. Vindication in one instance. Not everything but one thing out of many. Oh sweet hope restored! Where you see one injustice corrected you can hope for more. Honestly, this is not all about Walmart (only a little) but about things too precious to air here, not the least of which is "where is the healing?" He continues to show up in spite of my childishness. Probably because a hoard of prayer warriors keep praying while I'm having a melt down. Thank you Thank you Thank you.

Please press like when you have prayed.

#prayforBert #prayersmatter #Godisgood #winning #bleepbleepbleep #thecourtroomofjustice #hesthegoodjudge #imnottryingtoripyouoff #praisepays #3mileislandmeltdown

30

I Have Something to Contribute

There are different kinds of gifts, but the same Spirit.
There are different kinds of service, but the same Lord. There
are different kinds of working, but the same God works all of
them in all men . . . All these are the work of one and the same
Spirit, and he gives them to each one, just as he determines.
1 Corinthians 12:4-6; 11

My grandkids love to help cook. Whether it's stirring the batter,
breaking the eggs, turning the pancakes, or slicing the strawberries
- they love being part of the creation of a meal. There is a real
sense of accomplishment in being part of excellence. My daughter
has done an excellent job of equipping those kids to produce
culinary delights. She has empowered them year by year to handle
increasingly difficult aspects of meal preparation - never pushing
them beyond their ability but consistently setting the bar higher as
they mature. Even though it would be far easier, quicker, and
neater to do it herself, she makes sure they all get the opportunity
to participate.

As a pastor, part of the job is to attend conferences. Conferences
for training, conferences for equipping, conferences for connection,
conferences for further education, conferences to remind you of
what you already know but forgot. Lots and lots of conferences.
One of my favorites, though, has been the Leaders Advance at
Bethel Church in Redding. It features some of the top speakers of
our network speaking to leaders about leading. One Spring, Bert
and I were fortunate to be able to attend the advance together,
which was not always possible because of his job. The speakers

were targeting transition, which was very key for us at the time. I was so glad to have Bert there to help me process what we were hearing.

Toward the end of one of his messages, one of the speakers sensed the Holy Spirit wanted to heal disease, so he called for anyone in the conference with a life-threatening illness to stand and receive prayer. As Bert stood, several people gathered around him to minister. The woman next to him also stood up, and another group of people gathered around her. When the speaker called for prayer, Bert began praying for the woman next to him.

I was distressed beyond words! My reaction may sound a little crazy, but all I could think was, "He's acting as a drainpipe of healing! It's just passing through him to her." I wanted to jerk his hand off of her shoulder and place it on his abdomen. Just then, the Lord spoke to me, "Leave him be."

I, of course, began to argue. "But Lord, he needs all the healing he can get, and he's not receiving just giving."

"Nancy, no one likes to be in need all the time. Sometimes they need to know they have something to bring to the table. They have value. They are gifted and anointed. Bert can heal as well as be healed. Tonight, he needs to be the blessing. Leave him alone."

I believe we are wired to want to contribute, and when we aren't allowed to participate in a safe place actively, we get out of alignment. When children are forced to perform before they have been equipped or empowered, quite often, they develop a self-made/self-protective shell. As adults, they find it hard to receive. They are like orphans in the spirit - refusing to trust and embracing independence. I don't need you to pray for me - I will pray for you. When children only receive attention, and they can't contribute, their lack becomes their reward. They love being the center of attention, always seeking prayer or counsel, their neediness becoming their identity. When children have everything done for them, being excused from responsibility, they grow into entitled adults with the assumption that it's everyone else's responsibility to continue the cycle. I'm not saying this always happens, but, in my experience, it occurs more often than not.

Of course, Bert is none of these. He has gladly received prayer many times, but on this night, he felt like it was his time to contribute. I had allowed my desperation to "save" him to almost rob him of the joy of healing someone else.

I think this sheds some light on why God has determined to partner with humanity. Why, when it is clear that he is complete in himself and doesn't need us, he encourages us to get in the game — even waiting for our buy-in before he makes a move. I think it has to do with that same sense of value that my grandchildren experience in the kitchen. That same sense of value Bert felt praying for the woman next to him. How wonderful to be able to witness healing, a miracle, or salvation and be able to say, "I was part of that."

We've all experienced times when we didn't feel valued. Situations when we felt like we were observers at someone else's party or not even invited to the party. When we felt unqualified, disqualified, overlooked, or unseen. Take a few moments with Jesus and ask him if there is anyone in your life - past or present - that has made you feel that way. As names come to your mind, release each person into God's hands. Ask Jesus to cleanse your heart of any residual sense of shame, lack, or unforgiveness relating to that person or event. Take your time dealing with each occurrence.

Now, press into Jesus and ask him this: "Lord, what makes me special to you? What do I have to offer for the kingdom?"

Make a list of all the things he says about you. Read them out loud. Say them to yourself at least once a week. Post a list on your bathroom mirror and your refrigerator. Take up to a week to strengthen your confidence. Then become intentional about getting in the game, making a contribution, stirring the batter, so to speak, because everybody gets to play in the kingdom.

Prayer Illustration

Lord Jesus, Thank you for inviting me to partner with you. I pray your truth about me will release me from the lies that have kept me from participating in the growth of your kingdom. Please continue to remind me of who you say I am. In Jesus' name, Amen.

Excerpt from my Facebook timeline:
7/21/2018
Daily prayer reminder
One of the downsides of fighting this disease is that people begin to identify you with it. In other words the first thing they think of is that you are fighting this disease, not how amazing you are or that you have a whole life going on. Conversations center around the disease as everyone is concerned and wants to be brought up to date. But, honestly sometimes you don't want to talk about cancer. Sometimes you want to talk about anything but cancer. Of course we know people are just showing their love and concern but always talking about cancer means your focus is always

directed back to cancer. We're want our focus to be "other" directed which is why bert loves going to work. It gives him something else to focus on. If you talk to Bert this week, tell him you're praying for him and ask about his work, the church, the kids, or something else. There is so much more to him (and me) than cancer.

Please press like when you have prayed and feel free to share with praying friends or copy and paste.

#prayforBert #prayersmatter #godisgood #winning #imprayingforyou #howsyourgolfscore #howmuchmoneydoyoumake #howdidyouattractsuchahotwife #goodquestionstoask

31

The Assassin of Destinies

When Herod realized that he had been outwitted by the Magi,
he was furious, and he gave orders to kill all the boys in
Bethlehem and its vicinity who were two years old and under,
in accordance with the time he had learned from the Magi.
Matthew 2:16

Do you remember the movie "Minority Report" starring Tom
Cruise? It was a futuristic film where the authorities apprehend
criminals based on foreknowledge provided by psychics. Because of
the future forecast by their clairvoyants, a special force of the police
department can anticipate murder before it occurs and prevents it
by arresting the murderer before they can commit the crime. They
are basically re-writing someone's future by anticipating their
potential for violence. I believe this is the same tactic the devil uses.
He targets children with devastating lies as early as possible to
"arrest" them from who God created them to be. It's a strategy to
keep us from living to the fullness of the destiny for which God
created us. He is, quite literally, a destiny abortionist seeking to kill
our kingdom purpose before it is birthed.

As I've sought to move forward following Bert's death, I've
discovered so many things within me that needed to be exposed and
healed. Flaws that his presence in my life helped to cover up. It's as
if I used his love for me like a crutch enabling me to ignore broken
parts of myself. Being Mrs. Bert Boyd gave me a sense of
significance that I didn't believe I had apart from him. Most of my
self-value came from his value for me. In his absence, I was left
floundering for a sense of purpose and direction for my life.

Suddenly the lies that I'd managed to work around were glaringly exposed.

One of the most significant lies is based on the thought "I don't believe I'm good enough." I was surprised when God revealed this to me because I can be quite proud. (I almost wrote "vain" instead of "proud," but I'm too proud to admit to vanity.) However, when you consider that pride comes from repeatedly recounting your accomplishments to yourself to convince yourself you are good enough, you see how these two concepts go hand in hand.

Because this lie was rooted so deeply in my core, it had many toxic tendrils that branched out from it. As I mentioned, pride was easily identifiable. A lack of expectation to be paid was another. For most of my career as a pastor, I've worked for minimal pay, turning down increases in favor of bigger budgets for other items. The fact that Bert was well paid enabled me to act out of this core belief and camouflage it as generosity. Quite often, when people would offer to pay me for speaking, performing a wedding or something similar, I would respond, "Oh you don't need to pay me. I'm happy to do this." I thought I was being motivated by generosity, but the truth was I didn't believe I was worth paying. All the while, the people I was serving took me at my word, "I'm happy to do this for free." They didn't hear what I was not saying, "If I were good enough, you would force your money on me." The sad thing is I would often be angry and disappointed at how much work I ended up investing in the project with little to no appreciation expressed. I had arranged my circumstances to underscore my core belief.

We all like to believe we are open-minded. Unfortunately, this is not true. Our minds work very hard at maintaining what we already believe, even if it's a lie. Three people can invite you to lunch, but it is the one person who didn't include you that you will focus on because it reinforces the core belief that you are unwanted. That is how a lie becomes entrenched in our minds as truth. Once we accept a lie as truth, our brain works against us.

One of the most damaging tendrils of this core belief was that I didn't have as much anointing as other leaders in our stream - because I'm not good enough. This felt especially true following the death of my husband. Never mind the scores of healings that I'd seen or the miracles I'd participated in. Forget all the prophetic words and the transformed lives. None of these amounted to much in light of my failure to heal my own husband. In response to this tendril of thought, I found it harder and harder to connect with the voice of the Holy Spirit, which is so important to overcome a lie!

Even though I felt disconnected, I wasn't really. In truth, I was hearing from God very well. It was his voice that was exposing this lie and all its branches. As I actively sought to take my thoughts captive, I asked Holy Spirit what the source or root of me believing I was less anointed than others. He highlighted this lie to me in response, "You don't think you're good enough."

"What is the source of that belief?"

I immediately knew in my spirit it had to do with my mom. I loved my mom, and she had many beautiful qualities. I will be the first to tell you she did the best she could to raise five kids as a single mom on a waitress's wages. But she was like every other person, flawed, and perhaps her most significant flaw was she used her affection to manipulate your behavior. If you were compliant with what she wanted you to do, she showered you with love. If not, she withheld her love until you caved. I was applying my mom's behavior to the Holy Spirit. Since, in my core, I believed I was less than good enough, it felt quite logical to expect God to withhold his love (in the form of anointing) from me.

The next question was obviously, "why do I believe I'm not good enough?" I remembered that my oldest brother had died right after I was born from a brain aneurism. My next eldest brother had told me what our home was like at that time. My mom was devastated and became like a zombie in caring for most of her children. She was able to provide the basics, but we were not nurtured or comforted ourselves. Providing for any emotional need except her own was beyond her ability at that time.

I can only imagine how an infant would process the lack of attention from their primary caregiver. "I'm not good enough to warrant affection" was the lie the devil planted in my soul during that time. I'm not good enough to hold, snuggle, coo over. I'm fed and clean, but I must be missing something that would merit the attention I instinctively craved.

Of course, all of that information came to me in an instant. I asked, "If that is the lie, what is the truth?" I had a picture of my children come to mind. Each so different with their own personalities, strengths, and weaknesses and felt my heart swell with love.

"Do you love any one of these more or less than the others?"

"No. I am closer to some, but that's because they've chosen to be close to me. I would love to have that same closeness with each one."

"Is one of them better than the others?" "No."

"Have they earned your love by being good enough?" "Of course not."

"If your resources were unlimited, is there something you would do for one but not the others?" "Definitely not."

"If you love your children without condition, what makes you think I would place conditions on my love? Just as your mother's heart for your children wants only the best for them, so it is with my heart! I love you; I'm for you. I'm withholding nothing from you. You are more than enough just as you are."

I would love to say I've been instantly set free from that lie. I haven't been, but I'm learning to walk in the truth without Bert as my crutch. It's a process, but every day I feel like I've made headway. By the way, feel free to expect to pay me for services provided.

Prayer Illustration

Holy Spirit, please reveal any core lie I've been conditioned to believe. What is the source of that lie? Are there any other lies branching off from that lie? How have these lies played out in my life? What is your truth? Is there anyone I need to forgive or any soul ties that need to be cut? Please show me how to replace each lie with your truth. In Jesus's name, Amen. (If you find you are unable to see much progress on your own, you may consider seeking the assistance of a counselor, life coach, or inner healing ministry.)

Excerpt from my Facebook timeline:

5/16/2018

Daily Prayer reminder

My son in law and I were talking about the healing ministry yesterday and how almost every great faith healer has had someone close to them suffer devastating medical conditions or has suffered themselves. Yet, because of their perseverance in this ministry, countless others have been healed. I believe the devil recognized the threat that their faith represented and made it his assignment to discourage them before they realized their destiny and potential. I also believe that there should be many more believers walking in this ministry but that the devil was successful in his assignment and they believed the lie that healing people wasn't their call. Sometimes we see cancer or other diseases healed in an instant and other times it's a prolonged battle. I think the difference is whether we are simply facing a disease or an assignment meant to cancel out the potential of the people it is impacting. We do not discount evangelists when they have unsaved loved ones. No, we recognize the attack their family is under. In the same way, if you or someone you love have suffered, do not discount your potential as a healer. Someone is trying to stop you before you get started. Bert had 2 strangers tell him they saw an assignment for death upon him at the last leaders advance. This sounds scary but it's not. It simply confirms what we already knew. The good news is by the blood of Jesus we have the authority to cancel that assignment and bring charges against the enemy who issued it. The strategy of the enemy is often to attack the very thing you were meant to carry.

Please press like when you have prayed and feel free to share with praying friends or copy and paste.

#prayforBert #godisgood #prayersmatter #winning #thedevilplaysdirty #wearehealers #hesthegoodandjustjudge #justicecoming

32

Assignment Versus Disease

Put on the full armor of God so that you can stand against
the tactics of the Devil. Ephesians 6:11

I believe one of the greatest hindrances to the healing ministry is
the question: Why doesn't everyone get healed?

Bethel Church in Redding holds a special conference twice a year
for leaders who are affiliated with their network. It is a wonderful
time of relationship, encouragement, and equipping. At the last
meeting Bert attended, he went up front near the stage to worship
during the music. Jubilant but tired, he returned to our seats. It
was a delight to see his love for God radiate.

Ian Carroll was sitting behind us. I'd met Ian the day before. He
is an apostolic leader from the Chicago area and was in California
to teach a series in San Diego. He leaned forward and asked if Bert
was with me. I responded affirmatively, and he spoke to Bert.

"Sir, I must tell you that I see the devil has an assignment on your
life. He's trying to kill you."

Initially, Bert didn't hear him. He was leaning over, listening to
the woman seated next to him. She was a pastor from Texas. What
was she saying? She saw a demonic assignment on Bert to take his
life. Nearly word for word the same observation as Ian, although
neither of them knew of Bert's diagnosis.

Let me explain my understanding of a "demonic assignment."
They weren't saying that Bert had demons! A demonic assignment
is like a mob boss putting out a "hit" in the mafia. Everyone in his
"family" is charged with bringing about the death of the designee.
Both Ian and the Texas pastor wanted to make Bert aware, so he

knew to fight back. They were unaware that we had been fighting for over a year and a half.

This encounter affirmed what God had shown me at the beginning. Countless demons lined up to assault Bert's health and take his life. Before this, I hadn't put language around the picture, but "demonic assignment" fit like a glove. This encounter caused me to formulate a theory. Nothing I can prove. I don't even know if it's theologically sound, but I'm going to take a risk and share it with you. It has helped me to have a sliver of understanding, but I give you permission to reject it.

Why is it that I've prayed with some people, and they are suddenly healed? Torn ligaments restored, broken bones mended, eyesight restored - I've seen all of these things happen after praying. I believe we are witnessing the truth of "by his stripes we are healed." In other words, when we are only contending with disease and infirmity, the healing is instantaneous because Jesus paid the price to set us free from all diseases.

Then some people don't receive immediate healing but have a breakthrough after many prayers. I haven't been party to as many of these, although often I will have to pray two or three times with a person before they experience complete healing. Sometimes there are underlying issues that we're unaware of that hinders the healing. Whenever the person I'm praying with receives any measure of healing, our next prayer will be one of them giving thanks. Giving thanks is such an expression of faith and draws an increase in the spirit. It's often after giving thanks for the measure that we see the completion of healing.

Finally, there are people like Bert who don't see victory this side of heaven. I believe this may be because we are not battling a disease but an assignment. Some people persevere past the devils assigned to them, and some people, like my love, get worn down by the persistence of their enemy. This conflict is not a skirmish but a prolonged assault - a siege - in which many great people of faith succumb to the promise of heaven over the hell they are enduring. I am reminded of Ephesians 6:12. Although this scripture is traditionally used to caution us from seeing people as the enemy, I believe it applies to the healing ministry also.

As Paul wrote, "Our struggle is not against flesh and blood . . . " Because Jesus has secured our victory, we don't have to fight disease (flesh and blood). Our struggle is against the demonic realm " . . . but against the rulers, against the authorities, against the powers of this dark world and against the spiritual forces of evil in the heavenly realms." Ephesians 6:12

It's just a theory, but, for me, it is a small piece to the puzzle of why everyone isn't healed. Ultimately though, I accept that it continues to be a mystery this side of heaven. I look forward to the day the mystery is solved, but until then, I plan on contending for everything that Jesus won for us, especially healing.

Prayer Illustration

Father God, I see you in everything Jesus did. I know you are compassionate, loving, and faithful. The things I am facing today are in contradiction with what I know to be right about you. Today, I choose to believe in the Father Jesus revealed over the circumstances I don't understand. In Jesus' name, Amen.

Excerpt from my Facebook timeline:

2/10/19

Daily prayer reminder

Two years ago, someone asked me if it's always God's will to heal, why do people still die of cancer? My response was that I thought perhaps the people praying didn't realize their inheritance of power and authority over sickness. In retrospect, my answer seems to me a little insensitive. I regret that. That was of course before my own life was touched by cancer. So now I will respond from hopefully a more sensitive position. My answer - I don't know. I don't know why cancer continues to decimate bodies and ravage minds. I don't know why the thousands and thousands of prayers prayed for one man have not prevailed against this disease. I just don't know so I choose to focus on what I do know. There is not one good thing I could wish for Bert Boyd that isn't in the heart of God who is the source of goodness. If I am grieved by his suffering, how much more so is he grieved, who chose to give up heaven to physically suffer on behalf of humanity? I don't know what has kept the miraculous from manifesting for us, but I know miracles are possible because we have witnessed them and expect to continue to witness them. I know this is not God's will and he didn't design it for his purposes. Nothing this evil could have originated in heaven. I know my response to this moment in our lives is more important than having an explanation. It will determine the what and how of my future. I choose faith in the Father God that Jesus revealed when he healed everyone who came to him. I choose to trust in the heart that wept at the tomb of Lazarus. Dear ones, thank you for your faith and prayers. We love you for them.

#prayforBert #prayersmatter #godisgood #winning #itshiswillthatweovercome #lifeabundant

33
Restoration

I belong to my beloved, and his desire is for me.
Song of Solomon 7:10

Following Bert's death, I would have long conversations with Father God about my loneliness, fears, and the future. The business of dealing with death was lengthy and time-consuming. It was also exhausting and exasperating. Overwhelmed, I would take my frustrations to Father God and ask him to help me, protect me, and provide for me. Once, during this time, I wondered why all of my conversations were with the Father and not Jesus. I've always felt closer to Jesus, but I hadn't talked to him much since Bert's passing. I concluded I must need the protection of the Father at this time more than the companionship of Jesus and set the thought aside.

A little over six months after Bert's passing, I took a once in a lifetime trip to Israel with a group led by Stacey and Wesley Campbell and Brian and Candice Simmons. What an opportunity! Going to Israel was pretty low on Bert's bucket list (he was more like Mr. Hawaii), but I'd wanted to go for a long time. Who better to go with than Bible Scholars and Prophets? Initially, I was terrified of making the arrangements on my own, but I managed them and found myself in Israel. The tour was fantastic. Our guide was a Messianic Jew who also served the Israeli Special Forces. Between his background and the teaching of our leaders, this trip was better than I could have ever anticipated.

I have never been especially concerned about Israel politically. I just wanted to see what Jesus saw and walk where Jesus walked. As our guide shared the history of his people and their conflicts, his love for his country was compelling. I could understand why so many Christians are passionate Zionists (although I still felt no compulsion to buy a star of David to go with the cross on my necklace). Contemplating the history just given by our guide, I stood atop the Golan Heights, looking down upon the Valley of Tears. From our position, you could see the border fence with Israel on one side and Jordan on the other, and the contrast between the two countries immediately struck me. On Israel's side was agriculture - cultivated fields - right up to the border. Everything looked green and orderly and, honestly, prosperous. On the other side of the border were random trees or occasional bushes but no investment of seed or labor. It was almost as if you could see God's hand of favor resting upon this tiny country.

As I stood there, I felt a presence near me. In my mind's eye, I could see Jesus standing next to me. I heard, "I love this country," and I experienced a deep and penetrating sense of love touched with sorrow wash over me. It was as if I felt what he felt, and I was a little surprised at the intensity of the feeling. After all, isn't this the country of his crucifixion? But in an instant, I knew that wasn't what he was seeing. He saw the land he grew up in. The land he LIVED in. As understanding began to form in my mind, I heard, "I love these people." Again, I thought, aren't they the people who rejected him, who killed him and persecuted those that loved him? But I heard him say, "These are my kinsmen, my cousins, my brothers and sisters, my aunts, uncles, and parents. I love these people." Once again, a sense of love tinged with pain washed over me, and I was aware of a love that was profound and tangible. It made my heart ache to experience it. Everything in me felt that palpable love mingled with sadness.

It took my breath away. Then I could see Jesus turn to me as he said, "This is also how I love you." Up until that moment, I'd been swept up in experiencing his heart. I'd never had such an intimate encounter before. But when he said those words to me, it was as if I'd been dropped into ice water and before I could even think I responded, "I don't believe you. If you loved me, I would not be standing here alone." I turned and got back on the bus, leaving him behind.

The encounter and my response to it left me swimming. I tuned out the tour guide and everyone around me as I tried to process what I'd just experienced. Wave upon wave of pain and grief crashed in on me as I sat on that bus, trying to ignore Jesus.

Pictures were flashing through my mind of Martha and Mary after the death of Lazarus. Martha was grieved but not shaken. She had always seen Jesus as the Lord to serve, not the Lord who serves. But Mary. Mary was shaken to the core. She thought she was especially loved by this man/God who invited her into the inner circle. This Jesus, who valued her, included her in his thoughts and allowed her the place of favor at his feet. His failure to respond to her call meant much more than losing her beloved brother. It said she wasn't worth showing up for. He was still Lord, and she would come when he called, but she came as one unloved and abandoned, not the intimate and beloved friend she'd thought she was. She still believed in Jesus as God but had lost the innocence of knowing him as her beloved. I knew how she felt. I'd felt unique, precious, and valued. "If you loved me, I wouldn't be here alone," I thought again.

Yes, I could see all of this in my mind. In the Gospel of John, Mary's love is restored with the resurrection of Lazarus. "But there is no resurrection for me," I thought, heartbroken — no third-day miracle. I had pushed Jesus away when Bert died and I didn't want to hear from him. All that day and the next, I would listen to, "I love you," and I rejected it over and over again. I wasn't going to walk away from Christianity but I was changed. Something precious had died inside of me. I'd lost my innocence of faith.

"No thank you, sir. Keep your love. I'm just the hired help." I would say. Still, he kept coming. Popping into my thoughts throughout the day, "I love you. I love you. I love you." The more he said it, the deeper my pain. No wonder I'd only been praying to Father God. My disappointment with Jesus, the healer, was too great. I was heartbroken at the knowledge that my faith was so bruised I was incapable of trusting him.

On the day we were to be baptized in the Jordan River, I'd decided my baptism would be for the restoration of the innocence I'd lost. As I stepped in the shallow edge of the river and walked around, my friend and I laughed to feel the little fish there nibbling at our feet. After taking pictures for many of my friends, I decided to get in line to be baptized. As I was waiting I could feel the little fish nip, nip, nip, kiss, kiss, kiss all around my feet. It's kind of an irritating ticklish feeling. Soon my feet were surrounded by these little creatures all nip, nip, nipping, kiss, kiss, kissing. (I would like to interject that I'd gotten a pedicure just before the trip, and my feet were not crusty!) I was becoming reasonably self-conscious about it, especially when no one else in line had any fish around their feet. It was so unusual looking to see all these little fish swarming around my feet that my friend, Angela, took a picture for me. I progressed forward and was baptized by Stacey and Wesley Campbell. I went to the dressing room to change. I didn't feel any different, and I was disappointed. Coming out, Angela showed me the picture she'd gotten of the fish and commented that it must have been significant - a God moment. So I asked Jesus, was there any significance to the little fish bites.

He responded, "From the moment you stepped into the water, I didn't stop kissing your feet."

It took me a moment to process that. As I considered what Jesus said, I thought of the story of the woman who kissed and wept over his feet. Wow. What God does that? What kind of God humbles himself to kiss the feet of one so unworthy in order to win back her love? "I love you. I love you. I love you." I was awash in the love of this bridegroom. The innocence of my faith being tenderly restored through the kisses of the fish of the Jordan River.

When I fell in love with Jesus, I knew he forgave me my sins. He forgave me because he loved me. However, I really had no concept of the magnitude and intimacy of his love until I physically experienced it sweep over me on the Golan Heights. I did not comprehend the immensity of what it means to be loved by a God who is willing to die for you (let alone kiss your toes). Even now, I know I've only seen a glimpse of his love but that glimpse is enough to satisfy me. Jesus loves me. I think I believe it more now than I did before Bert died. With the knowledge of his love, came a restoration of faith and hope. I don't understand everything. I don't understand why the love of my life suffered and died and why we will not grow old together. I don't get it. Maybe in heaven, I will understand, but until then, I am choosing to trust. God is still good. We are still winning.

For this reason I kneel before the Father, from whom every family in heaven and on earth derives its name. I pray that out of his glorious riches he may strengthen you with power through his Spirit in your inner being, so that Christ may dwell in your hearts through faith. And I pray that you, being rooted and established in love, may have power, together with all the Lord's holy people, to grasp how wide and long and high and deep is the love of Christ, and to know this love that surpasses knowledge—that you may be filled to the measure of all the fullness of God.

Now to him who is able to do immeasurably more than all we ask or imagine, according to his power that is at work within us, to him be glory in the church and in Christ Jesus throughout all generations,

for ever and ever! Amen.

Ephesians 3:14-21